Greg Byrd, Lynn Byrd and Chris Pearce

Cambridge Checkpoint
Mathematics
Practice Book
9

CAMBRIDGE
UNIVERSITY PRESS

University Printing House, Cambridge CB2 8BS, United Kingdom

Cambridge University Press is part of the University of Cambridge.

It furthers the University's mission by disseminating knowledge in the pursuit of education, learning and research at the highest international levels of excellence.

www.cambridge.org
Information on this title: www.cambridge.org/9781107698994

© Cambridge University Press 2013

This publication is in copyright. Subject to statutory exception and to the provisions of relevant collective licensing agreements, no reproduction of any part may take place without the written permission of Cambridge University Press.

First published 2013
Reprinted 2013

Printed in the United Kingdom by Latimer Trend

A catalogue record for this publication is available from the British Library

ISBN 978-1-107-69899-4 Paperback

Cover image © Cosmo Condina concepts / Alamy

Cambridge University Press has no responsibility for the persistence or accuracy of URLs for external or third-party internet websites referred to in this publication, and does not guarantee that any content on such websites is, or will remain, accurate or appropriate.

Contents

Introduction		**5**
1	**Integers, powers and roots**	**7**
1.1	Directed numbers	7
1.2	Square roots and cube roots	8
1.3	Indices	9
1.4	Working with indices	10
2	**Sequences and functions**	**11**
2.1	Generating sequences	11
2.2	Finding the nth term	12
2.3	Finding the inverse of a function	13
3	**Place value, ordering and rounding**	**14**
3.1	Multiplying and dividing decimals mentally	14
3.2	Multiplying and dividing by powers of 10	15
3.3	Rounding	16
3.4	Order of operations	17
4	**Length, mass, capacity and time**	**18**
4.1	Solving problems involving measurements	18
4.2	Solving problems involving average speed	19
4.3	Using compound measures	20
5	**Shapes**	**21**
5.1	Regular polygons	21
5.2	More polygons	22
5.3	Solving angle problems	23
5.4	Isometric drawings	25
5.5	Plans and elevations	26
5.6	Symmetry in three-dimensional shapes	27
6	**Planning and collecting data**	**28**
6.1	Identifying data	28
6.2	Types of data	29
6.3	Designing data-collection sheets	30
6.4	Collecting data	31
7	**Fractions**	**32**
7.1	Writing a fraction in its simplest form	32
7.2	Adding and subtracting fractions	33
7.3	Multiplying fractions	34
7.4	Dividing fractions	35
7.5	Working with fractions mentally	36
8	**Constructions and Pythagoras' theorem**	**37**
8.1	Constructing perpendicular lines	37
8.2	Inscribing shapes in circles	38
8.3	Using Pythagoras' theorem	39
9	**Expressions and formulae**	**40**
9.1	Simplifying algebraic expressions	40
9.2	Constructing algebraic expressions	41
9.3	Substituting into expressions	43
9.4	Deriving and using formulae	44
9.5	Factorising	45
9.6	Adding and subtracting algebraic fractions	46
9.7	Expanding the product of two linear expressions	47
10	**Processing and presenting data**	**48**
10.1	Calculating statistics	48
10.2	Using statistics	50
11	**Percentages**	**52**
11.1	Using mental methods	52
11.2	Comparing different quantities	53
11.3	Percentage changes	54
11.4	Practical examples	55
12	**Tessellations, transformations and loci**	**56**
12.1	Tessellating shapes	56
12.2	Solving transformation problems	57
12.3	Transforming shapes	59
12.4	Enlarging shapes	60
12.5	Drawing a locus	61
13	**Equations and inequalities**	**62**
13.1	Solving linear equations	62
13.2	Solving problems	63
13.3	Simultaneous equations 1	64
13.4	Simultaneous equations 2	65
13.5	Trial and improvement	66
13.6	Inequalities	67
14	**Ratio and proportion**	**68**
14.1	Comparing and using ratios	68
14.2	Solving problems	70
15	**Area, perimeter and volume**	**72**
15.1	Converting units of area and volume	72
15.2	Using hectares	73
15.3	Solving circle problems	74
15.4	Calculating with prisms and cylinders	75
16	**Probability**	**76**
16.1	Calculating probabilities	76
16.2	Sample space diagrams	77
16.3	Using relative frequency	78
17	**Bearings and scale drawings**	**80**
17.1	Using bearings	80
17.2	Making scale drawings	82
18	**Graphs**	**83**
18.1	Gradient of a graph	83
18.2	The graph of $y = mx + c$	85
18.3	Drawing graphs	86
18.4	Simultaneous equations	87
18.5	Direct proportion	89
18.6	Practical graphs	90

19 Interpreting and discussing results **91**
19.1 Interpreting and drawing frequency diagrams 91
19.2 Interpreting and drawing line graphs 92
19.3 Interpreting and drawing scatter graphs 93
19.4 Interpreting and drawing stem-and-leaf diagrams 94
19.5 Comparing distributions and drawing conclusions 95

Introduction

Welcome to Cambridge Checkpoint Mathematics Practice Book 9

The *Cambridge Checkpoint Mathematics* course covers the Cambridge Secondary 1 Mathematics framework.

The course is divided into three stages: 7, 8 and 9. This Practice Book can be used with Coursebook 9. It is intended to give you extra practice in all the topics covered in the Coursebook.

Like the Coursebook, the Practice Book is divided into 19 units. In each unit you will find an exercise for every topic. These exercises contain similar questions to the corresponding exercises in the Coursebook.

This Practice Book gives you a chance to try further questions on your own. This will improve your understanding of the subject. It will also help you to feel confident about working on your own when there is no teacher available to help you.

There are no explanations or worked examples in this book. If you are not sure what to do, or need to remind yourself about something, look at the explanations and worked examples in the Coursebook.

1 Integers, powers and roots

◆ Exercise 1.1 Directed numbers

1. Work these out.
   a −6 + 2.7
   b −6 + −2.7
   c 16 + −2.7
   d 2.7 + −16

2. Work these out.
   a 7 − −5
   b 7.1 − −5.2
   c −7.1 − −5.2
   d −5.2 − −7.1

3. Work these out.
   a −8.4 + 12.1
   b −8.4 − 12.1
   c 8.4 − −12.1
   d −12.1 − −8.4

4. These are five temperatures, in degrees Celsius (°C).

   | 1.5 | −3.5 | −7 | −10 | −3 |

   Find the mean temperature.

5. Solve these equations.
   a $N + 2.3 = −4.7$
   b $2N + 6.8 = −10.2$
   c $N \div 4 = −2.7$

6. Work these out.
   a $−2 \times 3.4$
   b $−4.8 \div −4$
   c $−3 \times 9.2$
   d $14 \div −4$

7. Copy and complete this multiplication table.

×	−1.2	3
−1.1		
		−1.5

8. Use the information in the box to work out the value of each expression.
   a $r + s + t$
   b $(r − s) − t$
   c $(s − r) \times t$
   d $t \div (r − s)$
   e $(r + s) \div t$

   $r = 8.4 \quad s = 6.4 \quad t = −7.4$

9. $A + B = 0$ and $AB = −36$.
   What is the value of $A − B$?

Exercise 1.2 Square roots and cube roots

Do not use a calculator in this exercise, **except for questions 8 and 9.**

1 Estimate each root, to the nearest whole number.
   a $\sqrt{50}$ b $\sqrt{150}$
   c $\sqrt{350}$ d $\sqrt[3]{350}$

2 Explain why:
   a $\sqrt{95}$ must be between 9 and 10.
   b $\sqrt[3]{95}$ must be between 4 and 5.

3
$3 < \sqrt{10.5} < 4$

Write a similar statement for each of these roots.
   a $\sqrt{385}$ b $\sqrt[3]{500}$
   c $\sqrt{69.8}$ d $\sqrt[3]{55.5}$

4 a
$144 < N < 225$

What can you say about $\sqrt{N}$?

   b
$100 < M < 400$

What can you say about $\sqrt{M}$?

   c
$0 < R < 125$

What can you say about $\sqrt[3]{R}$?

5
$25.5^2 = 650.25 \quad 26.5^2 = 702.25$

   a Estimate $\sqrt{690}$ to the nearest whole number.
   b Estimate $\sqrt{650}$ to one decimal place.
   c Estimate $\sqrt{700}$ to one decimal place.

6 Show that $\sqrt[3]{200}$ is less than half $\sqrt{200}$.

7 a Show that $\sqrt{7500}$ is more than 80.
   b Show that $\sqrt[3]{7500}$ is less than 20.

8 Use a calculator to find the following square roots.
   a $\sqrt{30.25}$ b $\sqrt{441}$
   c $\sqrt{841}$ d $\sqrt{54.76}$
   e $\sqrt{174.24}$

9 Use a calculator to find the following square roots. Round your answers to two decimal places.
   a $\sqrt{6}$ b $\sqrt{60}$
   c $\sqrt{600}$ d $\sqrt{42.65}$
   e $\sqrt{2.43}$

Exercise 1.3 Indices

1. Write each number as an integer or a fraction.
   a 5^4
   b 3^5
   c 6^{-2}
   d 2^{-3}
   e 4^0

2. Write each number as a decimal.
   a 8^{-1}
   b 2^{-2}
   c 4^{-1}
   d 3^{-1}
   e 10^{-3}

3. Write these numbers in order of size, smallest first.

   1^{12} 2^6 3^4 4^3 6^2 12^1

4. Write these numbers in order of size, smallest first.

   1^{-5} 2^{-4} 3^{-3} 4^{-2} 5^{-1}

5. Write each number as a power of 4.
   a 16
   b 256
   c 1
   d $\frac{1}{4}$
   e $\frac{1}{64}$

6. Write each of the numbers in question **5** as a power of 2.

7. $3^N = 9^{-2}$
   Work out the value of N.

8. Write each expression as a single number.
   a $3^{-1} + 6^{-1}$
   b $4^2 + 4^1 + 4^0 + 4^{-1} + 4^{-2}$

Exercise 1.4 Working with indices

1 Simplify each expression.
Write the answers in index form.
  a $8^3 \times 8^2$
  b 7×7^3
  c $2^2 \times 2^2 \times 2^2$
  d $r^2 \times r^4$
  e $s^3 \times s^2 \times s$

2 Simplify each expression.
  a $4^2 \times 4^1$
  b 6×6^0
  c $c^2 \times c^2$
  d $\frac{1}{2} \times 2^5$
  e $e \times e^0$

3 Simplify each expression in the box. One is different from the other four. Which one?

  $a^4 \times a^2 \quad a^5 \times a \quad a^6 \times a^0$
  $a^0 \times a^5 \quad a^3 \times a^3$

  Give a reason for your answer.

4 This table shows powers of 9.

9^1	9^2	9^3	9^4	9^5	9^6
9	81	729	6561	59 049	531 441

Use the table to find the value of each expression.
  a $\sqrt{531\,441}$ b $\sqrt[3]{531\,441}$

5 Simplify each expression, writing it as a single power.
  a $a^5 \div a^3$
  b $6 \div 6^3$
  c $8^2 \div 8$
  d $d^2 \div d^2$
  e $e \div e^2$

6 Write each of these as a fraction.
  a $3^2 \div 3^4$ b $k^2 \div k^3$
  c $10^{-4} \times 10 \times 10$ d $4^2 \div 2^5$

7 Simplify each expression.
  a $\dfrac{a^3 \times a^2}{a}$ b $\dfrac{5^3 \times 5^3}{5}$
  c $\dfrac{f \times f^2}{f}$ d $\dfrac{10^3 \times 10^4}{10^2 \times 10}$

8 Find the value of n in each equation.
  a $5^n \times 5^3 = 625$ b $10^n \div 10 = 0.1$
  c $n^0 \times n^2 \times n = 64$

1 Integers, powers and roots

2 Sequences and functions

◆ Exercise 2.1 Generating sequences

1. Look at each sequence. Write down whether it is linear or non-linear.
   Explain your answers.
   - **a** 15, 19, 23, 27, 31, …
   - **b** 9, 10, 11, 12, 13, …
   - **c** 6, 7, 9, 12, 16, …
   - **d** 100, 93, 86, 79, 72, …
   - **e** 50, 46, 41, 35, 28, …
   - **f** 1, −2, −5, −8, −11, …
   - **g** $4\frac{1}{2}, 6, 7\frac{1}{2}, 9, 10\frac{1}{2}, …$
   - **h** 12.4, 11.3, 10.2, 9.1, 8, …
   - **i** −9, −4, 0, 3, 5, …

2. Write down the first four terms of each sequence described below.
   - **a** First term is 9, term-to-term rule is 'subtract 4'.
   - **b** First term is $1\frac{1}{2}$, term-to-term rule is 'add $1\frac{1}{2}$'.
   - **c** First term is −3, term-to-term rule is 'add 1, add 2, add 3, …'.
   - **d** First term is 10, term-to-term rule is 'subtract 1, subtract 3, subtract 5, …'.
   - **e** First term is 64, term-to-term rule is 'multiply by $\frac{1}{2}$'.
   - **f** First term is −64, term-to-term rule is 'divide by 2'.

3. Anders is trying to solve this problem.
   Work out the answer to the problem.
   Explain the method you used to solve the problem.

   The ninth term of a linear sequence is 32.
   The term-to-term rule is 'add 3'.
   Work out the fifth term of the sequence.

4. The sixth term of a non-linear sequence is 81.
   The term-to-term rule is 'multiply by 3'.
   Write down the first four terms of the sequence.
   Explain the method you used to solve this problem.

5. Use the position-to-term rule to work out the first four terms of each sequence.
   - **a** term = position number + 5
   - **b** term = position number − 7
   - **c** term = 2 × position number + 1
   - **d** term = position number^2 + 1
   - **e** term = position number^2 + 3
   - **f** term = position number^2 − 2
   - **g** term = 2 × position number^2
   - **h** term = 2 × position number^2 + 2

6. Use the position-to-term rules to work out:
   - **i** the first term
   - **ii** the second term
   - **iii** the tenth term of each sequence.
   - **a** term = 2 × position number + 3
   - **b** term = 5 × position number − 5
   - **c** term = 5 × position number^2
   - **d** term = position number^2 − 100

7. The position-to-term rule of a sequence starts: term = 5 × position number + ….
   The first term of the sequence is 9.
   Write out the complete position-to-term rule of the sequence.

8. The position-to-term rule of a sequence starts: term = position number^2 + ….
   The second term of the sequence is 7.
   Write out the complete position-to-term rule of the sequence.

Exercise 2.2 Finding the nth term

1. Work out the first three terms and the tenth term of each sequence.
   - **a** $5n$
   - **b** $n + 4$
   - **c** $2n + 8$
   - **d** $4n - 10$
   - **e** $10 - n$
   - **f** $2 - 10n$

2. Match each rectangular sequence card with the correct oval nth term expression card.

   | A −2, −1, 0, 1 | B 6, 9, 12, 15 | C 3, 6, 9, 12 | D 2, 1, 0, −1 | E 0, 3, 6, 9 |

   | i $n - 3$ | ii $3n$ | iii $3n - 3$ | iv $3n + 3$ | v $3 - n$ |

3. Work out an expression for the nth term for each sequence.
   - **a** 20, 22, 24, 26, ...
   - **b** 4, 6, 8, 10, ...
   - **c** 3, 11, 19, 27, ...
   - **d** −8, −4, 0, 4, ...
   - **e** 7, 6, 5, 4, ...
   - **f** 7, 4, 1, −2, ...
   - **g** 7, 0, −7, −14, ...
   - **h** −15, −10, −5, 0, ...
   - **i** −2, −3, −4, −5, ...

4. Use the nth term expression to work out the 20th term of each of the sequences in question **3**.

5. Look at this number sequence.

   20, 22, 24, 26, ...

   Explain why you can tell that the nth term expression for this sequence <u>cannot</u> be $5n + 15$, just by looking at the numbers in the sequence.

6. This pattern is made from grey squares.

   Pattern 1   Pattern 2   Pattern 3   Pattern 4

   Xavier thinks that the nth term for the sequence of numbers of grey squares is $4n - 3$.
   Is Xavier correct?
   Explain how you worked out your answer.

7. This pattern is made from black dots.

   Pattern 1   Pattern 2   Pattern 3   Pattern 4

   Razi thinks the expression for the nth term for the sequence of the number of black dots is $4n + 2$.
   Oditi thinks it is $6n$.
   Mia thinks it is $3n + 3$.
   Dakarai thinks it is $2n + 4$.
   Who is correct?
   Explain how you worked out your answer.

2 Sequences and functions

Exercise 2.3 Finding the inverse of a function

1. Work out the inverse of each function.
   a $y = x - 8$ **b** $y = x + 8$ **c** $y = 8x$ **d** $y = \frac{x}{8}$

2. Work out the inverse of each function.
   a $x \to x + 7$ **b** $x \to x - 7$ **c** $x \to 7x$ **d** $x \to \frac{x}{7}$

3. Work out the inverse of each function.
   a $y = 3x - 4$ **b** $y = 4x + 3$ **c** $y = \frac{x}{3} + 4$ **d** $y = \frac{x+3}{4}$

4. Work out the inverse of each function.
   a $x \to 2x + 5$ **b** $x \to 5x - 2$ **c** $x \to \frac{x}{2} - 5$ **d** $x \to \frac{x+5}{2}$

5. This is part of Alicia's homework.

   Question What do you notice about the inverse function of $x \to 9 - x$?
   Answer $x \to 9 - x$ is the same as $x \to -x + 9$

   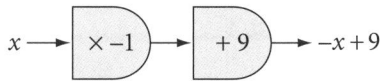

   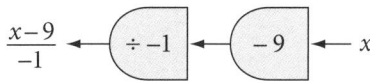

   $\frac{x-9}{-1}$ is the same as $\frac{9-x}{1}$ which is written as $9 - x$.
   The inverse function of $x \to 9 - x$ is $x \to 9 - x$.

   This is a *self-inverse* function.

   a Use Alicia's method to work out the inverse of each function.
     i $x \to 5 - x$ **ii** $x \to 3 - 3x$ **iii** $x \to 100 - x$ **iv** $x \to 4 - 7x$
   b Which of the functions in part **a** are self-inverse functions?

6. Sasha thinks of a number.
   She adds 1 to her number then multiplies the result by 5.
   a Use a mapping to write this as a function.
   The answer Sasha gets is 11.
   b Use inverse functions to work out the number Sasha thought of in the beginning. Show all your working.

7. Jake thinks of a number.
   He subtracts 3 from his number then divides the result by 4.
   a Use a mapping to write this as a function.
   The answer Jake gets is 2.25.
   b Use inverse functions to work out the number Jake thought of in the beginning. Show all your working.

3 Place value, ordering and rounding

◆ Exercise 3.1 Multiplying and dividing decimals mentally

1 Work these out mentally.
   a 4 × 0.3   b 13 × 0.2   c 4 × 0.9   d 0.9 × 9   e 0.3 × 11
   f 8 × 0.03 g 14 × 0.02 h 15 × 0.03 i 0.02 × 70 j 0.05 × 111

2 Work these out mentally.
   a 6 ÷ 0.3   b 8 ÷ 0.2   c 18 ÷ 0.6 d 28 ÷ 0.7 e 20 ÷ 0.1
   f 5 ÷ 0.02 g 9 ÷ 0.03   h 30 ÷ 0.01 i 36 ÷ 0.18 j 48 ÷ 0.12

3 Arrange these cards into groups that have the same answer.

   A 0.006 × 4   B 40 × 0.06   C 0.004 × 6   D 4 × 0.06

   E 0.04 × 0.6   F 0.6 × 4   G 0.4 × 0.6   H 0.4 × 6

   I 0.4 × 0.06   J 0.006 × 40 K 600 × 0.004 L 6 × 0.04

4 Which is the correct answer, A, B, C or D?
   a 0.9 ÷ 0.03 =   A 300   B 30   C 3   D 0.3
   b 3.5 ÷ 0.5 =   A 0.7   B 7   C 70   D 700
   c 0.08 ÷ 0.004 = A 2000   B 200   C 20   D 2
   d 0.25 ÷ 0.05 =   A 0.5   B 5   C 50   D 500

5 Work these out mentally.
   a 0.6 × 0.2   b 4.5 × 0.3   c 0.18 × 0.4   d 0.06 × 2.5   e 0.11 × 0.5
   f 0.6 ÷ 0.02 g 2.7 ÷ 0.3   h 0.45 ÷ 0.09 i 0.28 ÷ 0.04 j 3.6 ÷ 0.09

6 This is part of Hassan's homework. He has made some jottings to help him answer the question. Hassan has made a mistake. Explain the mistake he has made and work out the correct answer.

   Question Work $\frac{2.5 \times 0.2}{5 \times 0.1}$ out mentally.
   Answer   Top: 5.0 Bottom: 50   5 ÷ 50 = 0.1

7 Work out the answers to these questions mentally. Use jottings to help.
   a $\frac{16 \times 0.2}{0.02 \times 8}$ b $\frac{1500 \times 0.03}{7.5 \times 0.2}$ c $\frac{0.25 \times 100}{0.002 \times 25}$ d $\frac{80 \times 0.2 \times 0.2}{40 \times 0.4}$

8 a Work these out mentally.
     i 11 × 0.1   ii 11 × 0.2   iii 11 × 0.3   iv 11 × 0.4   v 11 × 0.5   vi 11 × 0.6
   b If you multiply a number by 0.9, would the answer be larger or smaller than when you multiply the number by 0.3? Look at your answers to part a, to help you decide.

9 a Work these out mentally.
     i 8 ÷ 0.1   ii 8 ÷ 0.2   iii 8 ÷ 0.4   iv 8 ÷ 0.5   v 8 ÷ 0.8
   b If you divide a number by 0.6, would the answer be larger or smaller than when you divide the number by 0.7? Look at your answers to part a, to help you decide.

Exercise 3.2 Multiplying and dividing by powers of 10

1 Work these out.
   a 28×10^2
   b 2.8×10^4
   c 28×10
   d 2.88×10^3
   e 2.8×10^5
   f 0.02×10^1
   g 28×10^0
   h 2×10^{-1}
   i 2.8×10^{-2}
   j 2800×10^{-4}
   k 28×10^{-3}
   l 288×10^{-1}

   Remember:
   $10^0 = 1$
   $10^1 = 10$

2 Work these out.
   a $34 \div 10$
   b $340 \div 10^2$
   c $34 \div 10^3$
   d $340 \div 10^4$
   e $0.34 \div 10^1$
   f $3400 \div 10^5$
   g $34 \div 10^0$
   h $0.34 \div 10^{-1}$
   i $34 \div 10^{-2}$
   j $3.04 \div 10^{-4}$
   k $0.03 \div 10^{-3}$
   l $0.034 \div 10^{-4}$

3 Copy this table, which is a secret coded message.

_	_	_	_	_	_		_	_		_	_	_		_	A	_	_	!
1.2	5	0.12	0.05	2000	0.2		5	0.5		12	0.05	50		0.05	500	0.2	0.02	

   Work out the answers to the calculations in the code box on the right.
   Find the answer in your secret code table. Write the letter from the code box above the number in your table.
   For example, the first calculation is $500 \div 10^0$.
   $500 \div 10^0 = 500$, so write A above 500 in your table.
   What is the secret coded message?

   $500 \div 10^0 = A$ $50 \times 10^{-3} = E$
   $0.05 \div 10^{-1} = F$ $0.5 \times 10^2 = N$
   $50 \times 10^{-1} = O$ $12 \div 10^1 = P$
   $0.2 \div 10^{-4} = R$ $200 \times 10^{-3} = S$
   $1200 \times 10^{-2} = T$ $0.12 \times 10^0 = W$
   $200 \div 10^4 = Y$

4 Work out the missing power in each of the questions in these spider diagrams.
   In each part, all the questions in the outer shapes should give the answer in the centre shape.

   a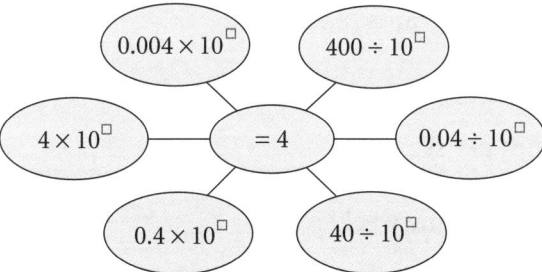
   b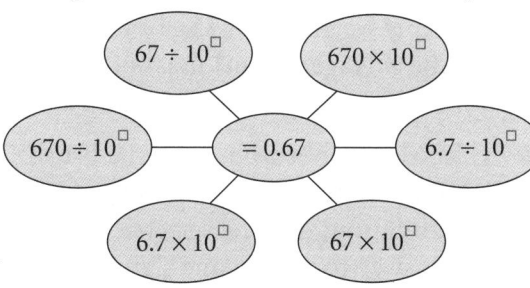

5 a Work these out.
   i 5×10^3 ii 5×10^2 iii 5×10^1 iv 5×10^0 v 5×10^{-1} vi 5×10^{-2}
   b Use your answers to part **a** to answer this question.
   If you multiply a number by 10^{-4}, would the answer be larger or smaller than when you multiply the number by 10^{-5}?

6 a Work these out.
   i $99 \div 10^3$ ii $99 \div 10^2$ iii $99 \div 10^1$ iv $99 \div 10^0$ v $99 \div 10^{-1}$ vi $99 \div 10^{-2}$
   b If you divide a number by 10^{-4}, would the answer be larger or smaller than when you divide the number by 10^{-5}? Look at your answers to part **a**, to help you decide.

3 Place value, ordering and rounding

Exercise 3.3 Rounding

1. Round each number to the given degree of accuracy.
   a 21.68 (one decimal place)   b 18.552 (two decimal places)   c 0.8466 (three decimal places)
   d 0.9915 (two decimal places) e 9.595959 (four decimal places) f 34.58955 (three decimal places)

2. Round the number 73.9530174 to the given number of decimal places (d.p.).
   a 1 d.p.   b 2 d.p.   c 3 d.p.   d 4 d.p.   e 5 d.p.   f 6 d.p.

3. Round each number to the given number of significant figures (s.f.).
   a 2468.15 (1 s.f.)   b 759.233 (2 s.f.)   c 5.3691 (3 s.f.)
   d 0.0781 (1 s.f.)   e 0.1954 (2 s.f.)   f 6.03888 (3 s.f.)

4. Which is the correct answer, **A, B, C** or **D**?
   a 567 rounded to 1 s.f. is   **A** 5   **B** 6   **C** 500   **D** 600
   b 15.493 rounded to 2 s.f. is   **A** 15   **B** 16   **C** 15.49   **D** 15.50
   c 0.07887 rounded to 3 s.f. is   **A** 0.078 **B** 0.079 **C** 0.0789 **D** 0.0790
   d 0.0077777 rounded to 4 s.f. is   **A** 0.0077 **B** 0.0078 **C** 0.007777 **D** 0.007778

5. Round the number 254059.9524 to the given number of significant figures (s.f.).
   a 1 s.f.   b 2 s.f.   c 3 s.f.   d 4 s.f.   e 5 s.f.   f 6 s.f.
   g 7 s.f.   h 8 s.f.   i 9 s.f.

6. Gina drove from her house in Madrid to a friend's house in Paris, a distance of 1275.3 km.
   She then drove to another friend's house in Rome, a distance of 1445.2 km.
   How far did Gina drive altogether?
   Give your answer correct to two significant figures (2 s.f.).

7. Instructions on a packet of rice suggest serving 75 g per person.
   Yuang carefully weighed out 75 g of rice, and counted 2896 grains of rice.
   Work out the average (mean) mass of a single grain of rice.
   Give your answer correct to three significant figures (3 s.f.).

8. Gerry's electric toothbrush rotates the brush 125 times per second.
   Gerry brushes her teeth for two minutes, twice a day.
   How many rotations does her electric toothbrush make in one week?
   Give your answer correct to one significant figure (1 s.f.).

9. Complete these steps for each part, below.
   i   Work out an estimate of the answer by rounding each number to one significant figure.
   ii Use a calculator to work out the accurate answer. Give this answer correct to three significant figures (3 s.f.).
   iii Compare your estimate with the accurate answer to help you decide if your accurate answer is correct.

   a 0.6292×189.3 b $782.5 \div 1.95$ c 21.4×590

   d $\dfrac{0.7951 \times 206}{1.96}$ e $\dfrac{9732 - 3176}{6.816}$ f $\dfrac{48.22 + 9.81}{20.05}$

   g $\dfrac{158.2}{0.1956 \times 43.5}$ h $\dfrac{2.104 \times 11.795}{7.887 - 3.109}$ i $\dfrac{78\,500 \times 0.02}{0.235 \times 388}$

◆ Exercise 3.4 Order of operations

1 Work these out.
  a $20 + 2 \times 4$ **b** $15 - 5 \times 2$ **c** $10 \times 2 + 5$ **d** $3 \times 3 - 3$ **e** $8 + \frac{12}{4}$
  f $18 - 10 \div 2$ **g** $2 \times 6 - 3 \times 4$ **h** $\frac{30}{10} + \frac{30}{5}$ **i** $3 \times 7 - \frac{4}{2}$ **j** $2(22 + 9)$
  k $5 + 3^2$ **l** $4^2 + 5^2$ **m** $5^2 - 2(12 - 9)$ **n** $2 \times 3^2 - 1$ **o** $1 - 2^2 + 3 \times 4$

2 Write the correct sign, =, < or > to go in the box between the expressions in each pair.
  a $60 - 20 \times 2 \;\square\; 30 + \frac{24}{6}$
  b $100 - 8^2 \;\square\; 4(70 - 61)$
  c $4^2 + 3^2 + 2^2 + 1^2 \;\square\; 8^2 - 6^2$
  d $12 \div 6 + \frac{60}{6} \;\square\; 21 - 5 \times 2^2$
  e $8 + 4(4 + 4) \;\square\; 2(6^2 - 20)$
  f $(5 + 4)^2 \;\square\; 7^2 + \frac{64}{2}$

3 Check the answers to these calculations and decide whether they are right (✓) or wrong (✗). If the answer is wrong, write down the correct answer.
  a $6 + 3 \times 2 = 18$
  b $3(16 - 3^2) + 9 = 30$
  c $5 - (8 - 6)^3 = 27$
  d $\frac{20}{4} - 3^2 + 2(3 + 12) = 26$
  e $(1^2 - 2^2 + 3^2)^2 = 12$
  f $24 \div (2 + 2^2) = 16$

4 This is part of Shen's homework.

Question Work these out.
  a $5 + 5 \times 5$ **b** $10(14 - 3^2)$ **c** $\frac{20 - 6}{6 + 1}$

Answer
  a $5 + 5 = 10,\; 10 \times 5 = 50$
  b $14 - 3 = 11,\; 11^2 = 121,\; 121 \times 10 = 1210$
  c $20 - 6 \div 6 + 1 = 20 - 1 + 1 = 20$

All of his answers are wrong. For each part:
  i explain the mistake that Shen has made
  ii work out the correct answer.

5 Harsha and Ahmad are trying to work out the value of the expression $2(3x + 2y)$ when $x = 3$ and $y = 7$. Read what they are saying.

I think the answer is 120 because $33 + 27$ is 60, then $2 \times 60 = 120$.

I think the answer is 154 because $3 \times 3 = 9,\; 9 + 2 = 11$, then $11 \times 7 = 77$ and $2 \times 77 = 154$.

Is either of them correct?
Explain your answer.

6 Work out the value of each expression when $x = 3$ and $y = 4$.
  a $2x + y^2$ **b** $3x^2 - 5y$ **c** $(2x + y)^2$ **d** $10(5x - 3y)^2$

3 Place value, ordering and rounding

4 Length, mass, capacity and time

◆ Exercise 4.1 Solving problems involving measurements

1 A recommended portion of Lee's muesli weighs 75 g.
   Lee's muesli contains 71% wheat and oats, 26.5% fruit and 2.5% nuts.
   a What is the mass of wheat and oats in one portion of Lee's muesli?
   b What is the mass of nuts in one serving of Lee's muesli?

   For each question in this exercise, show all your working and check your answers.

2 A carton of orange juice holds 2 litres.
   Dean and his wife each drink a 200 ml glass of orange juice a day.
   Their daughter drinks a 150 ml glass of orange juice a day.
   How many days will a full carton of orange juice last?

3 Fitta spends 25 minutes on his rowing machine every day,
   except at weekends.
   How long will Fitta spend on his rowing machine in
   four weeks?
   Give your answer in hours and minutes.

4 This chart shows the distances, in miles, between some towns in the USA.

Fort Collins				
102	Sterling			
303	366	Grand Junction		
64	127	243	Denver	
65	178	307	146	Laramie

   For example, this box shows that the distance between Sterling and Laramie is 178 miles.

   Duke delivers furniture. Last week he drove:
   • from Fort Collins to Sterling and back twice
   • from Fort Collins to Grand Junction, on to Denver, on to Laramie, then straight back to Fort Collins.
   Work out the total distance, in kilometres, that he drove last week.

5 The diagram shows part of a kitchen floor.
   Eva has put down three rows of tiles across the width of the kitchen.
   Each square tile is 17.5 cm wide.
   Between the tiles she puts a layer of glue 4 mm thick.
   a Work out the total length of the floor that Eva's three rows of
      tiles cover so far. Give your answer in centimetres.
   Eva's kitchen is 2.1 m long.
   b How many more rows of tiles does she need to lay to reach the end of the kitchen?

   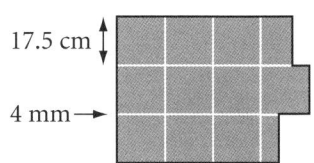

6 Bim plans to sell cups of hot chocolate at a charity swim.
   Bim has a hot water container that holds 14 litres.
   He needs about 220 ml of hot water for each cup of hot chocolate.
   a How many cups of hot chocolate can he make from a full container of water?
   Bim will charge $1.70 per cup of hot chocolate. He hopes to sell 200 cups of hot chocolate.
   b How many full containers of water will he use?
   c How much money will he make?

Exercise 4.2 Solving problems involving average speed

For each question in this exercise, show all your working and check your answers.

1. A car travels a distance of 174 km in 3 hours.
   What is its average speed?

2. Ariadne jogs at an average speed of 8 km/h.
   How far does she travel in $1\frac{1}{2}$ hours?

3. How long will it take a train to travel 50 km at an average speed of 40 m/s?
   Give your answer in minutes and seconds.

4. Alejandro has to go to a meeting in Santiago, Chile.
   This is 540 km from his home.
   He sets off from home at 6:15 a.m.
   He expects to drive at an average speed of 80 km/h for the journey.
   At what time does he expect to arrive in Santiago?

5. Felipe ran 10 km in 40 minutes.
   He rested for 5 minutes then ran a further 8 km in 35 minutes.
   Work out his average speed for the whole journey.
   Give your answer in kilometres per hour (km/h), correct to the nearest whole number.

6. Francisca lives 25 km from her place of work.
   Each day, she drives from home to work and back again.
   For 15 km of her journey, she travels along a quiet road at an average speed of 50 km/h.
   For 10 km of her journey, she travels along a busy road at an average speed of 30 km/h.

   a Work out the total time it takes her to get from her home to work each day.
   b Work out her average speed for the whole journey.
      Give your answer correct to the nearest whole number.

   Francisca works from Monday to Friday every week.

   c Work out the total time that Francisca spends travelling to and from work in one week.
      Give your answer in hours and minutes.

   To change a decimal or fraction of an hour into minutes, multiply by 60, for example:
   $\frac{1}{3}$ of an hour → $\frac{1}{3}$ × 60 = 20 minutes
   0.2 hours → 0.2 × 60 = 12 minutes
   To change minutes back to hours, divide by 60, for example:
   72 minutes → 72 ÷ 60 = 1.2 hours
   140 minutes → 140 ÷ 60 = $2\frac{1}{3}$ hours

7. The 100 m world record was completed at an average speed of 37.6 km/h.
   Work out this speed in metres per second (m/s).
   Give your answer correct to one decimal place (1 d.p.).

8. In Florida a captive cheetah was accurately measured running at 71 miles per hour.
   Work out the speed of this cheetah in metres per second (m/s).
   Give your answer to the nearest whole number.

9. A tortoise can reach speeds of 0.12 m/s.
   Work out the speed of a tortoise in kilometres per hour (km/h).

10. To get into orbit around the Earth, a space shuttle needs to be travelling at about 7780 m/s.
    Work out the speed of the space shuttle in miles per hour.
    Give your answer to the nearest hundred.

4 Length, mass, capacity and time

Exercise 4.3 Using compound measures

For each question in this exercise, show all your working and check your answers.

1. Aeroplane A travels 1220 km in $3\frac{1}{2}$ hours.
   Aeroplane B travels 830 km in $2\frac{1}{2}$ hours.
   Which aeroplane travels faster?

2. Greg has entered a cycle race of 125 km.
   He rides the first 85 km in $2\frac{1}{2}$ hours. He rides the rest of the way in 2 hours.
   How much faster did he ride during the first part of the journey compared to the second?

3. Lynn is training for a bicycle race. She cycles every Monday and Thursday.
   On Monday she cycled 85 km in 4 hours.
   On Thursday she cycled $52\frac{1}{2}$ km in 2 hours and 20 minutes.
   a Work out the speed that Lynn cycled each day.
   b On which day did Lynn cycle faster?

4. A pack of six pens costs $5.79. A pack of 20 of the same pens costs $19.70.
   a Work out the cost per pen for each pack.
   b Which pack is better value for money?

5. A 330 ml can of lemonade costs $0.49.
   A 2 litre bottle of the same lemonade costs $2.69.
   a Work out the cost for each in <u>cents per millilitre</u>.
   b Which is better value for money?

6. A 375 g box of breakfast cereal costs $1.65. A 650 g box of the same breakfast cereal costs $2.86.
   Which box is better value for money?

7. A 50 ml tube of toothpaste costs $0.79. A 175 ml tube of the same toothpaste costs $2.30.
   Which tube is better value for money?

8. Anna likes to solve crossword puzzles.
   It took her 10 minutes and 12 seconds to complete one puzzle with 34 clues.
   It took her 22 minutes to complete a different puzzle with 80 clues.
   a For each puzzle, work out how many seconds it took Anna to complete one clue.
   b Use your answer to part **a** to decide which crossword puzzle Anna found easier.

9. Rafael cycled to visit his grandmother.
   The travel graph shows his journey to and from his grandmother's house.
   He stayed with his grandmother for $1\frac{1}{2}$ hours before returning home.
   a Work out Rafael's average speed for:
      i   the journey to his grandmother's house
      ii the journey home from his grandmother's house.
   b During which part of the journey was Rafael travelling faster?
   c Work out Rafael's average speed for the whole journey.
      Give your answer correct to one decimal place (1 d.p.).
      Do not include the time he spent at his grandmother's house.

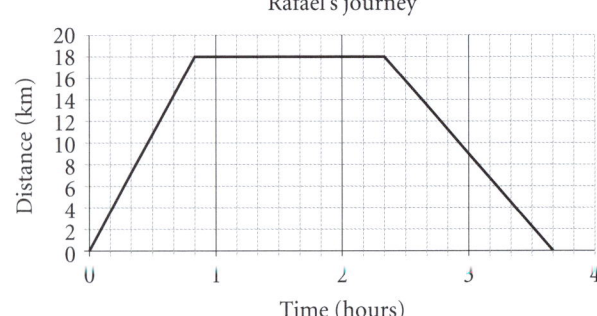

Rafael's journey

5 Shapes

◆ Exercise 5.1 Regular polygons

1. Show that the interior angle of a regular octagon is 135°.

2. Calculate the interior angle of a regular polygon with:
   a 12 sides   **b** 15 sides.

3. **a** Copy and complete this table to list the angles of regular polygons.

Number of sides	Exterior angle	Interior angle
5	72°	
10		
20		
40		

   b Look again at the table you completed in part **a**.
   If you double the number of sides of a regular polygon, what happens to the exterior angle?

4. **a** The exterior angle of a regular polygon is 20°.
      How many sides does the polygon have?
   b The exterior angle of a regular polygon is 18°.
      How many sides does this polygon have?

5. Work out the number of sides of a regular polygon, if the interior angle is:
   a 170°   **b** 172°   **c** 177°.

6. Can a regular polygon have an interior angle of:
   a 156°   **b** 132°?

   > Give reasons for your answers.

7. The diagram shows two sides of a regular polygon.

   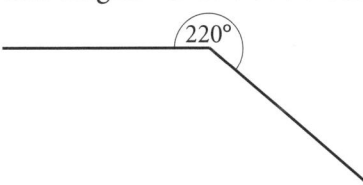

   How many sides does the polygon have?

8. The diagram shows a regular octagon and an equilateral triangle joined together.

   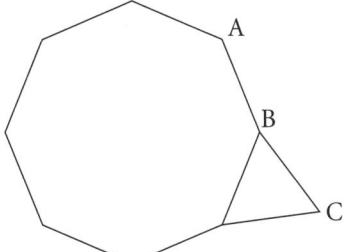

   AB and BC are two sides of a regular polygon.
   How many sides does this polygon have?

Exercise 5.2 More polygons

1. Work out the sum of the interior angles of:
   a an octagon
   b an 11-sided polygon
   c a 12-sided polygon.

2. Two of the angles of this polygon are 100°.
   All the other angles are equal.

   Calculate the size of the unmarked angles.

3. Maha has a square piece of card.
   She cuts off three of the corners.
   What is the sum of the angles of the card shape she has made?
   Give a reason for your answer.

4. Find the number of sides of the polygon, if the sum of the interior angles is:
   a 360°   b 720°   c 1440°.
   Give reasons for your answers.

5. Two of the interior angles of a hexagon are 100° and three are 150°.
   a Find the size of the sixth interior angle.
   b Show that the sum of the exterior angles is 360°.

6. a Show that 1980° could be the sum of the interior angles of a polygon.
   b What is the next number, after 1980, that could be the sum of the interior angles of a polygon?

7. Find the exterior angle at:
   a A   b E   c D.

   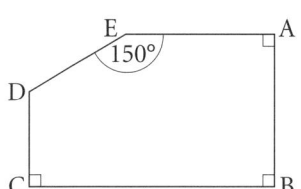

8. The smallest exterior angle of a polygon is 40°.
   The largest exterior angle is 80°.
   a What is the smallest possible number of sides?
   b What is the largest possible number of sides?

Exercise 5.3 Solving angle problems

1. In the diagram, PQ is parallel to ST.
   PRT and QRS are straight lines

   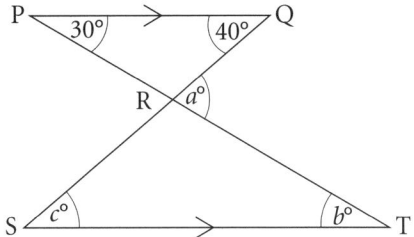

   > Give reasons for your answers in all the questions in this exercise.

   a Work out the value of a.
   b Work out the value of b.
   c Work out the value of c.

2. In the diagram, O is the centre of the circle.
   XY is a diameter.

   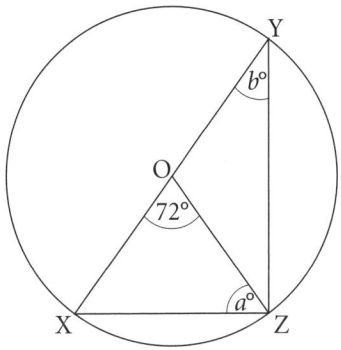

   a Work out the value of a.
   b Work out the value of b.
   c Work out the size of angle XZY.

3. This shape is a kite.

   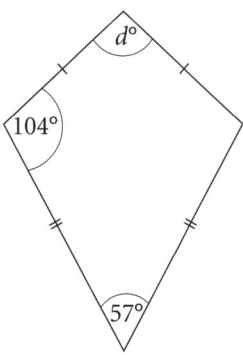

   Calculate the size of the angle labelled $d°$.

4 AB is parallel to DC.

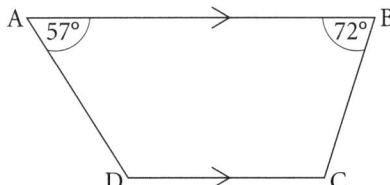

Calculate the sizes of the other two angles of the quadrilateral.

 5 Two squares and two equilateral triangles meet at a point.

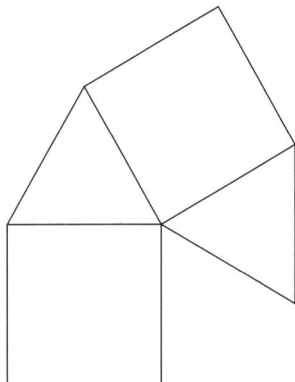

Show that an equilateral triangle will fit in the gap.

 6 Work out the sizes of the angles labelled $r°$, $s°$ and $t°$.

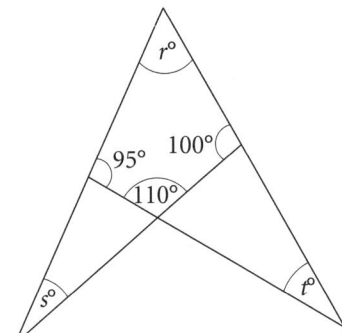

5 Shapes

Exercise 5.4 Isometric drawings

You need isometric paper for this exercise.

1 Use isometric paper to draw cuboids with edges of these lengths.

   a 3 cm, 3 cm and 2 cm   **b** 4 cm, 1 cm and 2 cm   **c** 6 cm, 3 cm and 1 cm

2 This is an isometric drawing of a cuboid.
  The length of the shortest edge is 14 cm.
  How long are the other edges?

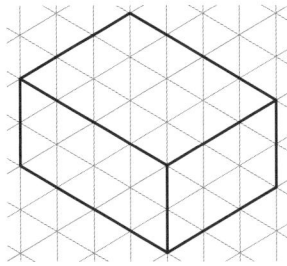

3 Pieter has a wooden cube. The length of each edge is 3 cm.
  Pieter cuts a square hole of side 1 cm all the way through the cube, through the centres of opposite faces. Pieter does this twice more, so that there is a hole through each face of the cube.
  Each face looks like this.

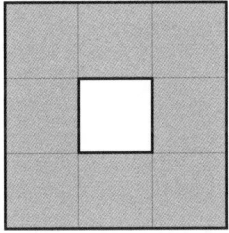

Draw the finished cube.
Use isometric paper.

4 Anders knows that he can join five squares to make C-shape or a T-shape.

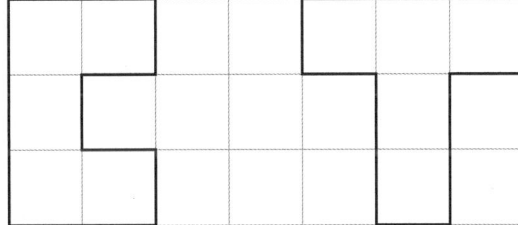

He makes each of these solid shapes by joining five cubes together.
Draw each shape.
Use isometric paper.

5 Pablo has a wooden cube.
  He has cut off one corner, so it looks like this.
  Draw two different diagrams of the shape.
  Use isometric paper.

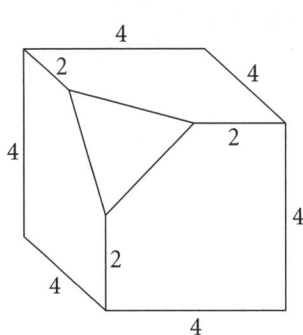

5 Shapes

Exercise 5.5 Plans and elevations

1 Look at these isometric drawings of three shapes.

You need isometric paper for this exercise.

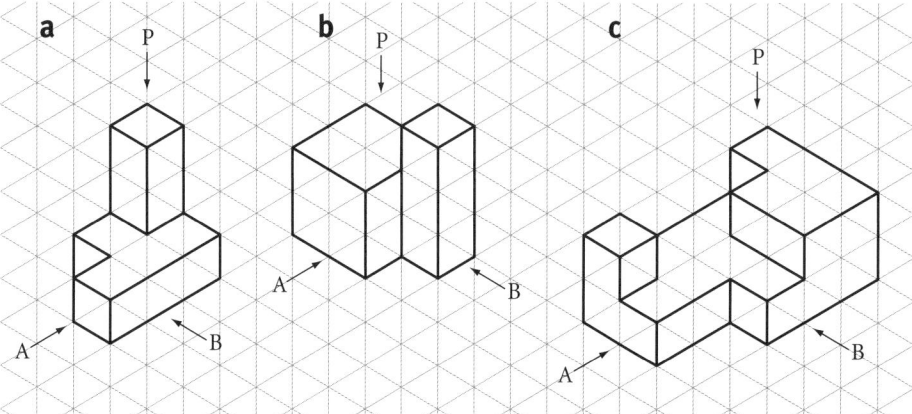

Draw a plan view (from P) and two elevations (from A and B) for each shape.

2 The diagram shows a plan and two elevations of a shape made by joining cubes together.

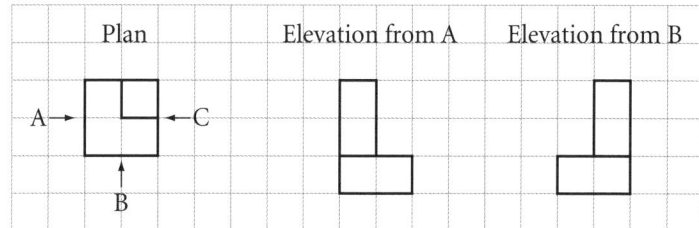

a Draw the elevation from C.
b Draw the shape on isometric paper.

3 A shape is made by joining cubes together.
The diagram shows a plan and two elevations for the shape.

a How many cubes are joined together?
b Draw the shape on isometric paper.

Exercise 5.6 Symmetry in three-dimensional shapes

1 Here are two isometric drawings of two prisms. Draw the plane of symmetry of each one.

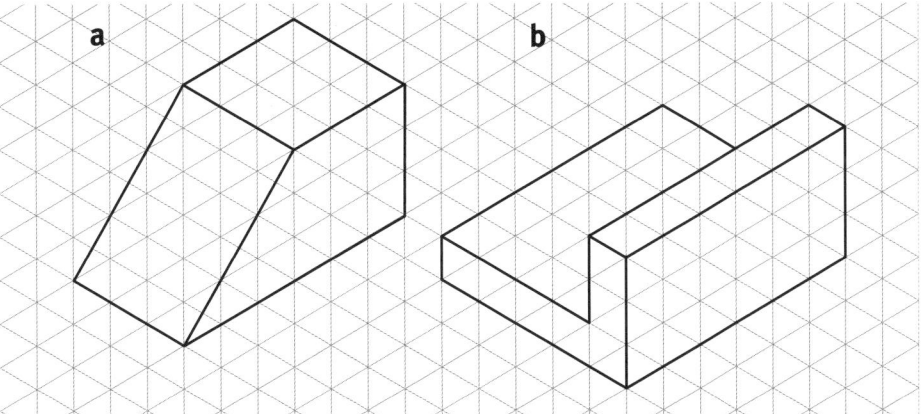

2 This is a cuboid.
It has five planes of symmetry. Draw diagrams to show them.

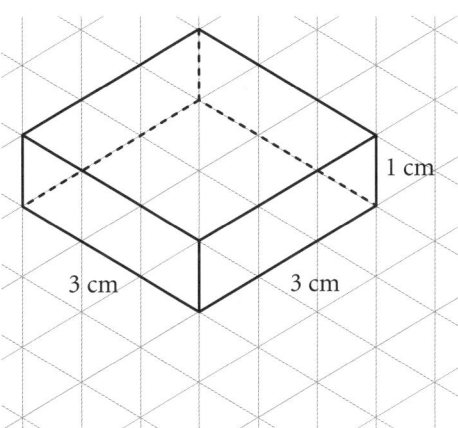

3 This is an isometric drawing of <u>half</u> a three-dimensional shape.
The shaded face is on the plane of symmetry.
Draw the whole shape.

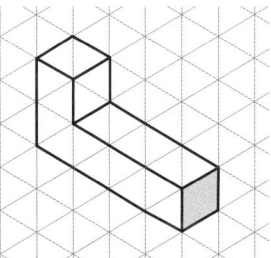

4 This is an isometric drawing of half a shape. The shaded face is on the plane of symmetry.
  a Draw the whole shape.
  b What is the name of the whole shape?

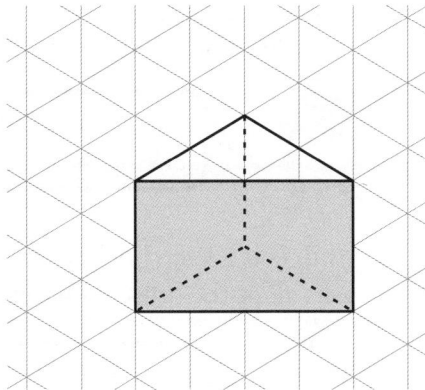

5 a How many planes of symmetry does a pyramid with a square base have?
  b Make sketches to show them.

5 Shapes

6 Planning and collecting data

◆ Exercise 6.1 Identifying data

1 Write a hypothesis for each investigation.
   a Razi wants to know whether more men than women like gardening.
   b Xavier wants to know if women think men with spiky hair look silly.
   c Sasha wants to know if girls are better than boys at texting quickly.
   d Dakarai wants to know if boys can throw a ball more accurately than girls can.
   e Tanesha wants to know whether good cooks go to restaurants more often than bad cooks.
   f Zalika wants to know if girls who drink lots of water have healthier skin than those who don't.

For questions **2** and **3**, remember to follow these steps.
   • Decide on a hypothesis to test.
   • Decide on the question, or questions, to ask.
   • Decide what data to collect.
   • Decide how to collect the data.
   • Decide how big the sample size will be.
   • Decide how accurate the data needs to be.

2 There are 750 students in Ahmad's school.
   Ahmad wants to know whether right-handed students are better at writing their name with their <u>left</u> hand than left-handed students are at writing their name with their <u>right</u> hand.
   a Write down examples for each of the six steps that Ahmad should follow.
   b What other factors could Ahmad consider?
   c Write down some problems Ahmad may have in collecting his data.

3 Harsha is reading a magazine.
   She wants to know whether there are usually more pictures in her dad's newspaper than in her magazine.
   a Write down examples for each of the six steps that Harsha should follow.
   b What other factors could Harsha consider?
   c Write down some problems Harsha may have in collecting her data.

4 For each part of this question, give a reason why the student cannot make the conclusion they have, and suggest a better sample that they could use.
   a Alicia wants to know whether boys eat more junk food than girls. She surveys all the students on her school bus. There are 22 boys and nine girls on her bus.

The boys ate more junk food than the girls, so the boys in the school eat worse food than the girls do.

   b Anders is a keen hockey player. He wants to know the favourite sport of the boys in his school. He asks all of the boys in his year group's hockey team about their favourite sport.

Most of the students who I asked said that hockey was their favourite sport. So the most popular sport of the boys in my school is hockey.

◆ Exercise 6.2 Types of data

1. Decide whether primary or secondary data should be used in each of these investigations. Give a reason for each answer.
   a Hassan is investigating whether members of his family think Barbados is a good holiday destination.
   b Maha is investigating whether numbers of flights to Lagos airport have increased in the last two years.
   c Mia is investigating whether 'Mia' is a common name in other countries.
   d Shen is investigating whether women's favourite flower is the rose.
   e Oditi is investigating the most popular model of motorcycle.
   f Jake is investigating how many people use a local supermarket.

2. Xavier wants to find out the most popular magazine that is sold in Madrid. He finds data that shows the most popular magazine that is sold in the tourist areas of Spain is the '¡Hola!' magazine. Read what he says.

> I can assume that ¡Hola! is also the most popular magazine that is sold in Madrid.

   a Explain why you think it is reasonable for Xavier to make this assumption.
   b Explain why you think that Xavier should <u>not</u> have made this assumption.

3. Sasha wants to find out the average price of a laptop computer in Mexico. She finds data that shows the average price of a laptop computer in the USA is $550.

> I can assume that the average price of a laptop computer in the Mexico is $550.

   a Explain why you think it is reasonable for Sasha to make this assumption.
   b Explain why you think that Sasha should <u>not</u> have made this assumption.

Exercise 6.3 Designing data-collection sheets

1. Tanesha carried out an experiment with an ordinary dice.

   I rolled the dice 100 times and recorded the number it landed on.

   Design a suitable data-collection sheet for Tanesha to use.

2. Razi surveyed the makes of motorcycles at a motorcycle show.

   I recorded the makes BMW, Ducati, Harley Davidson, Honda, Moto Guzzi, and 'Other'.

   Design a suitable data-collection sheet for Razi to use.

3. Mia wanted to know how many brothers students in her school had.

   I asked 100 students how many brothers they have.

   Design a suitable data-collection sheet for Mia to use.
   (Assume the highest number of brothers is four.)

4. Harsha is investigating the number of shoes owned by students at her college. She uses this data-collection sheet.

Number of pairs of shoes	Tally	Frequency
0		
5–10		
10 or more		
	Total	

   I asked 50 students to say how many pairs of shoes they own.

   a. Give two reasons why her data-collection sheet is not suitable.
   b. Design a better data-collection sheet for Harsha to use.

Exercise 6.4 Collecting data

1 Zalika rolled a four-sided dice 20 times.

I rolled the dice and recorded the numbers.

These are the numbers she rolled.

1	1	4	2	1	4	4	2	3	1
3	2	1	3	2	4	1	2	3	4

a Record this information on a data-collection sheet.
b Write down one conclusion that you can make from the results on your data-collection sheet.

2 These are the masses, to the nearest gram, of kittens born at a veterinary surgery in one week.

92	104	82	96	82	102	98	78	106	118
84	115	95	105	94	76	85	108	99	88

a Record this information on a data-collection sheet.
b Write down one conclusion that you can make from the results on your data-collection sheet.

3 These are the numbers of texts sent by a group of friends in one day.

16	22	38	2	14	35	18	36	25
28	8	12	25	0	12	31	5	45

a Record this information on a data-collection sheet.
b Write down one conclusion that you can make from the results on your data-collection sheet.

6 Planning and collecting data

7 Fractions

◆ Exercise 7.1 Writing a fraction in its simplest form

1 Write each fraction in its simplest form.
 a $\frac{6}{10}$
 b $\frac{16}{20}$
 c $\frac{15}{21}$
 d $\frac{24}{30}$
 e $\frac{24}{36}$
 f $\frac{150}{250}$

2 Write each fraction in its lowest terms.
 a $\frac{16}{32}$
 b $\frac{18}{81}$
 c $\frac{30}{36}$
 d $\frac{21}{49}$
 e $\frac{60}{144}$
 f $\frac{99}{121}$

3 Write each fraction in its lowest terms. Show how you check your answers.
 a $\frac{18}{45}$
 b $\frac{32}{48}$
 c $\frac{32}{56}$
 d $\frac{56}{96}$
 e $\frac{96}{120}$
 f $\frac{120}{220}$

Exercise 7.2 Adding and subtracting fractions

1. Work out these additions and subtractions.
   Write each answer in its simplest form and as a mixed number when appropriate.

   a $\frac{1}{4}+\frac{1}{8}$ **b** $\frac{1}{5}+\frac{7}{10}$ **c** $\frac{2}{9}+\frac{5}{18}$ **d** $\frac{8}{9}-\frac{2}{3}$ **e** $\frac{4}{7}-\frac{10}{21}$ **f** $\frac{7}{12}-\frac{1}{4}$

   g $\frac{2}{5}+\frac{3}{4}$ **h** $\frac{6}{7}+\frac{1}{2}$ **i** $\frac{5}{9}+\frac{13}{27}$ **j** $\frac{9}{13}-\frac{1}{2}$ **k** $\frac{5}{6}-\frac{3}{4}$ **l** $\frac{13}{16}-\frac{7}{12}$

2. Copy and complete these.

   a $4\frac{1}{3}+5\frac{6}{7}$ ① $4+5=9$ ② $\frac{1}{3}+\frac{6}{7}=\frac{\Box}{21}+\frac{\Box}{21}=\frac{\Box}{21}, \frac{\Box}{21}=1\frac{\Box}{21}$ ③ $9+1\frac{\Box}{21}=10\frac{\Box}{21}$

   b $8\frac{1}{4}-3\frac{9}{10}$ ① $\frac{33}{4}-\frac{39}{10}$ ② $\frac{33}{4}-\frac{39}{10}=\frac{\Box}{20}-\frac{\Box}{20}=\frac{\Box}{20}$ ③ $\frac{\Box}{20}=\Box\frac{\Box}{20}$

3. Work out these additions and subtractions.
   Write each answer in its simplest form and as a mixed number when appropriate.
   Show all the steps in your working.

   a $3\frac{5}{6}+\frac{1}{3}$ **b** $1\frac{1}{3}+7\frac{5}{12}$ **c** $5\frac{7}{8}+2\frac{1}{4}$ **d** $2\frac{3}{5}+\frac{5}{6}$ **e** $5\frac{7}{8}+2\frac{7}{12}$ **f** $3\frac{3}{4}+3\frac{3}{5}$

   g $7\frac{5}{7}-\frac{9}{14}$ **h** $5\frac{1}{3}-\frac{20}{21}$ **i** $7\frac{3}{10}-6\frac{4}{5}$ **j** $9\frac{1}{9}-3\frac{1}{3}$ **k** $6\frac{2}{5}-2\frac{1}{8}$ **l** $11\frac{1}{9}-1\frac{11}{12}$

 4. Read what Shen says.

> If I add together two mixed numbers, my answer will always be less than the sum of the whole-number parts plus 1.

Use at least two counter-examples to show that Shen's statement is not true.

 5. Xao is a plumber.
   He has two pieces of pipe.

   The first piece is $3\frac{2}{5}$ m long; the second is $4\frac{3}{4}$ m long.

   He fixes them together, as shown in the diagram.

   a What is the total length of the two pipes?

   Xao wants a pipe that is $10\frac{1}{4}$ m long.

   b How much more pipe does he need?
   c Show how to check your answer is correct.

 6. Silvie has a piece of wood $4\frac{1}{8}$ m long.

   She wants to make some shelves.

   She cuts two pieces of wood, each $1\frac{3}{4}$ m long, from the piece she has.

   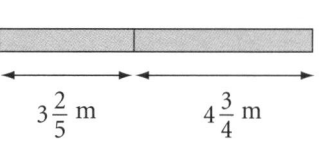

   a How long is the piece of wood that Silvie has left?
   b Show how to check that your answer is correct.

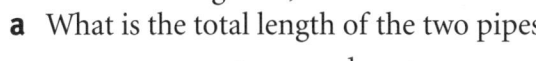

7 Fractions

Exercise 7.3 Multiplying fractions

1 Work out these multiplications.
Cancel common factors before multiplying.
 a $\frac{3}{5} \times 15$ b $\frac{3}{4} \times 16$ c $\frac{3}{5} \times 25$ d $\frac{3}{7} \times 77$ e $\frac{3}{13} \times 130$ f $\frac{3}{20} \times 220$

2 Work out these multiplications.
Cancel common factors before multiplying.
Write each answer as a mixed number in its simplest form.
 a $\frac{3}{8} \times 18$ b $\frac{4}{15} \times 35$ c $\frac{5}{12} \times 8$ d $\frac{6}{25} \times 55$ e $\frac{7}{20} \times 32$ f $\frac{8}{9} \times 24$

3 Work out these multiplications.
Cancel common factors before multiplying when possible.
Write each answer in its lowest terms.
 a $\frac{3}{5} \times \frac{6}{7}$ b $\frac{4}{5} \times \frac{7}{12}$ c $\frac{5}{6} \times \frac{7}{8}$ d $\frac{19}{20} \times \frac{5}{6}$ e $\frac{3}{4} \times \frac{7}{10}$ f $\frac{3}{4} \times \frac{12}{13}$
 g $\frac{6}{21} \times \frac{7}{18}$ h $\frac{3}{8} \times \frac{8}{15}$ i $\frac{21}{22} \times \frac{4}{6}$ j $\frac{8}{15} \times \frac{5}{24}$ k $\frac{5}{6} \times \frac{36}{55}$ l $\frac{9}{20} \times \frac{8}{15}$

4 Work out these multiplications.
Cancel common factors before multiplying when possible.
Write your answer as a mixed number in its simplest form.
 a $2\frac{1}{4} \times 1\frac{2}{5}$ b $1\frac{1}{4} \times 4\frac{1}{5}$ c $2\frac{1}{7} \times 2\frac{1}{6}$ d $5\frac{1}{2} \times 2\frac{4}{33}$
 e $2\frac{1}{5} \times 1\frac{1}{5}$ f $8\frac{1}{3} \times 2\frac{7}{10}$ g $10\frac{2}{5} \times \frac{25}{26}$ h $\frac{8}{9} \times 2\frac{5}{14}$

5 Read what Hassan says.

> If I multiply together two proper fractions, I will always be able to cancel the answer.

Use at least two counter-examples to show that Hassan's statement is not true.

6 a The guests at a party eat $\frac{3}{4}$ of the cakes. Yasmina eats $\frac{1}{4}$ of what is left.
What fraction of the cakes does Yasmina eat?
 b The guests at another party eat $\frac{9}{10}$ of a salad. Marie eats $\frac{2}{3}$ of what is left.
What fraction of the salad does Marie eat?

Exercise 7.4 Dividing fractions

1 Work out these divisions.
Write each answer in its simplest form and as a mixed number when appropriate.

   a $20 \div \frac{4}{7}$ **b** $21 \div \frac{7}{8}$ **c** $16 \div \frac{8}{11}$

   d $12 \div \frac{4}{9}$ **e** $30 \div \frac{2}{3}$ **f** $24 \div \frac{6}{7}$

   g $20 \div \frac{4}{5}$ **h** $14 \div \frac{8}{9}$ **i** $60 \div \frac{15}{22}$

   j $32 \div \frac{10}{11}$ **k** $6 \div \frac{4}{11}$ **l** $18 \div \frac{8}{9}$

2 Work out these divisions.
Write each answer in its lowest terms and as a mixed number when appropriate.

   a $\frac{3}{4} \div \frac{4}{5}$ **b** $\frac{5}{6} \div \frac{1}{5}$ **c** $\frac{9}{13} \div \frac{2}{5}$

   d $\frac{6}{7} \div \frac{4}{5}$ **e** $\frac{4}{9} \div \frac{2}{11}$ **f** $\frac{7}{10} \div \frac{1}{6}$

   g $\frac{5}{6} \div \frac{11}{12}$ **h** $\frac{3}{8} \div \frac{2}{9}$ **i** $\frac{32}{45} \div \frac{8}{15}$

   j $\frac{3}{4} \div \frac{3}{4}$ **k** $\frac{7}{12} \div \frac{21}{36}$ **l** $\frac{24}{25} \div \frac{16}{75}$

3 Work out these divisions.
Write your answer in its simplest form and as a mixed number when appropriate.

   a $2\frac{1}{2} \div 2\frac{3}{5}$ **b** $3\frac{3}{4} \div 1\frac{1}{5}$

   c $3\frac{1}{5} \div 5\frac{1}{3}$ **d** $4\frac{1}{3} \div 3\frac{1}{2}$

   e $4\frac{2}{3} \div 1\frac{1}{6}$ **f** $6\frac{2}{3} \div 2\frac{1}{7}$

   g $3\frac{3}{4} \div \frac{7}{12}$ **h** $\frac{4}{7} \div 2\frac{1}{4}$

4 Read what Maha says.

> If I divide a proper fraction by a different proper fraction, my answer will always be a proper fraction.

Use at least two counter-examples to show that Maha's statement is <u>not</u> true.

5 Work out these divisions.
Write your answer in its simplest form and as a mixed number when appropriate.
Show how you check your answers.

   a $\frac{1}{4} \div \frac{3}{5}$ **b** $\frac{4}{5} \div \frac{1}{6}$ **c** $\frac{4}{7} \div \frac{12}{13}$ **d** $\frac{9}{10} \div \frac{3}{4}$

◆ Exercise 7.5 Working with fractions mentally

1 Work out these additions mentally.

    a $\frac{1}{12} + \frac{1}{6}$ b $\frac{3}{4} + \frac{1}{12}$ c $\frac{3}{5} + \frac{1}{15}$ d $\frac{1}{10} + \frac{3}{5}$

    e $\frac{4}{5} + \frac{11}{20}$ f $\frac{1}{20} + \frac{1}{100}$ g $\frac{1}{2} + \frac{1}{3}$ h $\frac{1}{3} + \frac{1}{4}$

    i $\frac{1}{4} + \frac{1}{5}$ j $\frac{1}{2} + \frac{3}{5}$ k $\frac{3}{10} + \frac{3}{4}$ l $\frac{5}{6} + \frac{5}{8}$

> In all the questions in this exercise, write each answer in its simplest form and as a mixed number when appropriate.

2 Work out these subtractions mentally.

    a $\frac{1}{5} - \frac{1}{10}$ b $\frac{1}{10} - \frac{1}{30}$ c $\frac{1}{5} - \frac{1}{25}$ d $\frac{2}{5} - \frac{1}{15}$ e $\frac{5}{6} - \frac{5}{18}$ f $\frac{11}{15} - \frac{3}{5}$

    g $\frac{1}{2} - \frac{1}{5}$ h $\frac{4}{5} - \frac{3}{4}$ i $\frac{5}{9} - \frac{1}{2}$ j $\frac{6}{7} - \frac{3}{4}$ k $\frac{3}{4} - \frac{1}{6}$ l $\frac{7}{8} - \frac{5}{12}$

3 Work out these multiplications mentally. Use jottings if you need to.

    a $\frac{1}{3} \times \frac{1}{2}$ b $\frac{2}{3} \times \frac{1}{3}$ c $\frac{3}{4} \times \frac{3}{7}$ d $\frac{4}{5} \times \frac{3}{7}$ e $\frac{4}{9} \times \frac{5}{7}$ f $\frac{9}{20} \times \frac{9}{10}$

    g $\frac{1}{2} \times \frac{2}{5}$ h $\frac{3}{5} \times \frac{7}{12}$ i $\frac{5}{6} \times \frac{9}{11}$ j $\frac{3}{10} \times \frac{5}{9}$ k $\frac{3}{5} \times \frac{5}{6}$ l $\frac{9}{10} \times \frac{25}{33}$

4 Work out these divisions mentally. Use jottings if you need to.

    a $\frac{1}{4} \div \frac{1}{2}$ b $\frac{1}{16} \div \frac{1}{4}$ c $\frac{1}{9} \div \frac{1}{3}$ d $\frac{1}{8} \div \frac{3}{4}$ e $\frac{3}{4} \div \frac{1}{8}$ f $\frac{5}{8} \div \frac{5}{9}$

    g $\frac{5}{9} \div \frac{5}{8}$ h $\frac{9}{10} \div \frac{3}{7}$ i $\frac{3}{4} \div \frac{9}{11}$ j $\frac{9}{10} \div \frac{3}{5}$ k $\frac{5}{6} \div \frac{20}{21}$ l $\frac{10}{21} \div \frac{4}{15}$

> Work out the answers to **questions 5 to 8** mentally.
> Use jottings to help if you need to.

5 In a box of chocolates, $\frac{1}{5}$ are plain chocolate, $\frac{1}{3}$ are white chocolate and the rest are milk chocolate.
What fraction of the box of chocolates are milk chocolate?

6 In a bunch of flowers, $\frac{3}{5}$ are carnations, $\frac{1}{8}$ are roses and the rest are lilies.
What fraction of the bunch of flowers are lilies?

7 At a football game $\frac{2}{7}$ of the people watching are children.
$\frac{3}{8}$ of the children are girls.
    a What fraction of the people watching the football game are girls?
    b What fraction of the people watching the football game are boys?
    c What fraction of the people watching the football game are <u>not</u> children?

8 At a cat show $\frac{2}{7}$ of the people have brought at least one cat.
The rest are just watching.
$\frac{3}{5}$ of the people who are just watching are female.
    a What fraction of all the people at the cat show are female and are there just to watch?
    b What fraction of all the people at the cat show are there just to watch and are male?

8 Constructions and Pythagoras' theorem

◆ Exercise 8.1 Constructing perpendicular lines

1. Draw a line AB, 7 cm long.
   Mark the point C on the line, 2 cm from A.
   Construct the perpendicular at C, as shown in the diagram.

   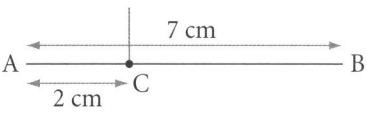

2. Draw a line PQ, 10 cm long.
   Mark points R and S on the line, each 4 cm from an end of the line, as shown.
   Construct the perpendicular at R and the perpendicular at S, as shown in the diagram.

   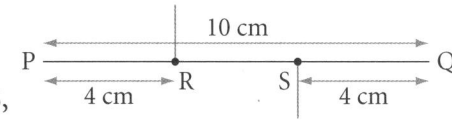

3. Construct a rectangle of length 7 cm and width 3 cm. Do not use a protractor.

4. Maha draws a horizontal line.
   Then she draws a line EF, 6 cm long, at an angle of 60° to the horizontal line.
   She constructs the perpendicular at F, which meets the horizontal line at G, as shown in the diagram.
   a Make an accurate copy of the diagram.
   You may use a protractor to draw the 60° angle, but not the perpendicular line.
   Maha says that angle EGF is 30°.
   b Show that she is correct by:
   i using a protractor to measure angle EGF on your drawing
   ii calculating angle EGF, using the facts that you know about the sum of the angles in a triangle.

   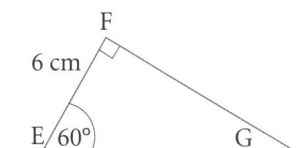

5. Copy the diagram, making it twice as large.
   On your copy, construct the perpendicular from the point P to the line.

6. Copy the diagram, making it twice as large.
   On your copy, construct the perpendiculars to the line from the points A and B.

   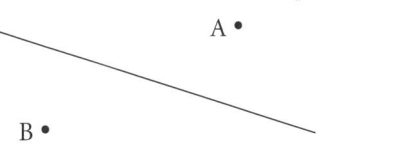

7. Anders draws a vertical line.
   He marks the points C and D at different distances to the right of the line.
   He constructs the perpendiculars from C to the line and from D to the line.
   He labels the points where they meet the line as A and B.
   Then Anders completes the quadrilateral ABCD, as shown in the diagram.
   a Make a copy of the diagram.
   Anders says that the sum of angles ADC and BCD is 180°.
   b Show that he is correct by:
   i using a protractor to measure angles ADC and BCD on your drawing and working out the total
   ii calculating the total of angles ADC and BCD, using the facts that you know about the sum of the angles in a quadrilateral.

   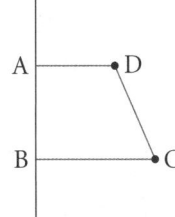

Exercise 8.2 Inscribing shapes in circles

1. For each part, draw a circle with a radius of 6 cm.
   Using a straight-edge and compasses, inscribe in your circle:
   a an equilateral triangle   b a regular octagon.

2. The diagram shows a square inscribed in a circle of radius 5 cm. 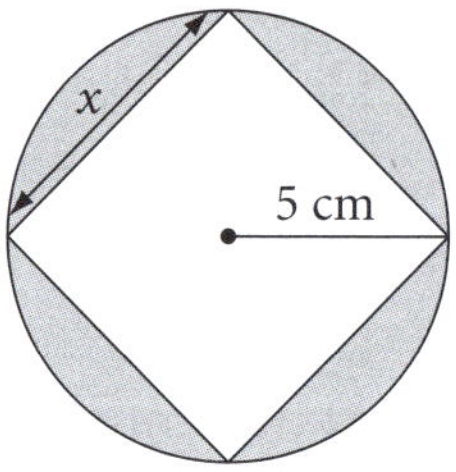
   a Make an accurate copy of the diagram.
   b Measure the length of the side of the square, marked x in the diagram.
      Write your measurement to the nearest millimetre.
   c Copy and complete the workings below to calculate the area of the shaded
      region in the diagram. Use $\pi = 3.14$.
      Area of circle: $\pi \times r^2 = \pi \times 5^2 = 78.5\,cm^2$
      Area of square: $x \times x = \Box \times \Box = \Box\,cm^2$
      Shaded area: area of circle – area of square $= 78.5 - \Box = \Box\,cm^2$

3. Ahmad wants to estimate the area of a hexagon inscribed in a circle of radius 7 cm.
   These are the steps he follows.

   Step 1 Draw a circle of radius 7 cm.
   Step 2 Construct an inscribed hexagon.
   Step 3 Draw a circle inside the hexagon that touches each side of the hexagon.
   Step 4 Measure the radius of the smaller circle.
   Step 5 Area of large circle $= \pi \times 7^2 = 153.86\,cm^2$
             Area of small circle $= \pi \times 6.1^2 = 116.84\,cm^2$
             The area of the hexagon must be bigger than $116.84\,cm^2$ but smaller than $153.86\,cm^2$. 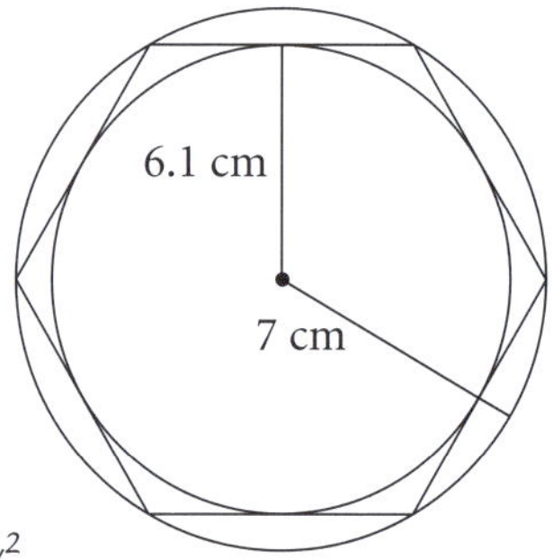
   Halfway between 116.84 and 153.86 is $\frac{116.84 + 153.86}{2} = 135.53$.
   I estimate the area of the hexagon to be $135\,cm^2$.

   Use Ahmad's method to work out an estimate for the area of an octagon inscribed in a circle of radius 7 cm.

4. Mia inscribes a square in a circle of radius 8 cm.
   Dakarai inscribes a square in a circle of radius 4 cm.

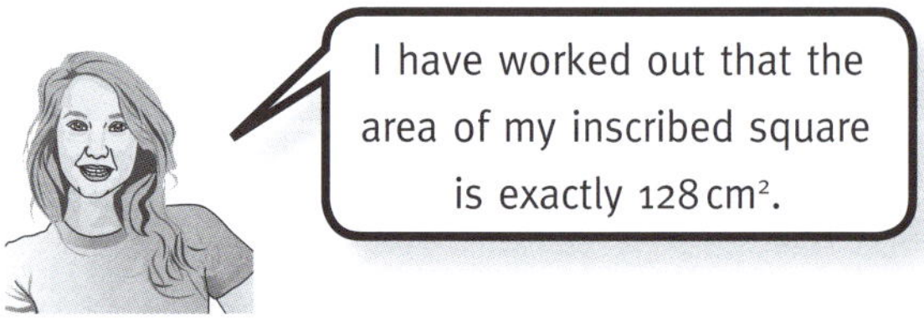

   > I have worked out that the area of my inscribed square is exactly $128\,cm^2$.

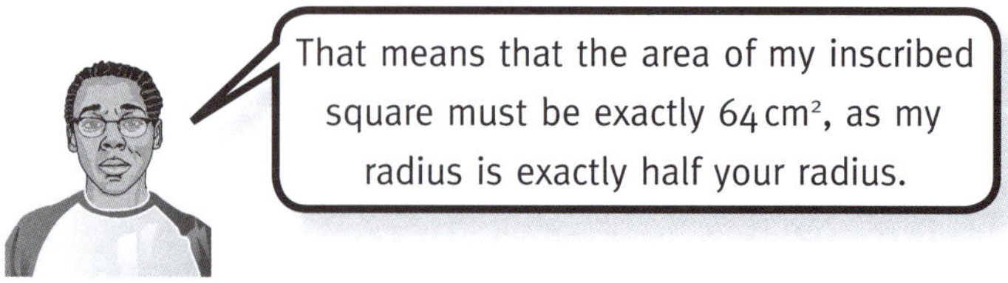

   > That means that the area of my inscribed square must be exactly $64\,cm^2$, as my radius is exactly half your radius.

   a Show that Mia's statement is true by drawing an accurate diagram.
   b How can you tell without drawing a diagram that Dakarai's statement is false?
   c Show that Dakarai's statement is false by drawing an accurate diagram.

Exercise 8.3 Using Pythagoras' theorem

1 Work out the length of the hypotenuse in each triangle.
 The first one has been started for you.

 a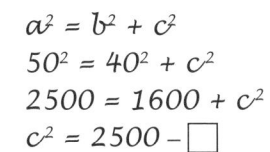
 $a^2 = b^2 + c^2$
 $a^2 = 10^2 + 24^2$
 $a^2 = 100 + 576$

 b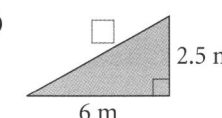

2 Work out the lengths of the sides marked □ in each triangle.
 The first one has been started for you.

 a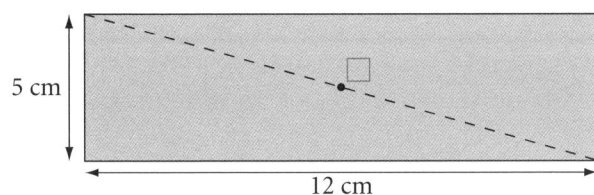
 $a^2 = b^2 + c^2$
 $50^2 = 40^2 + c^2$
 $2500 = 1600 + c^2$
 $c^2 = 2500 - \square$

 b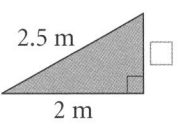

3 This rectangle has length 12 cm and width 5 cm.
 Work out the length of a diagonal of the rectangle.

 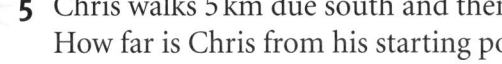

4 A square has a side length of 10 cm.
 Work out the length of a diagonal of the square.

 Draw diagrams to help you solve these problems.

5 Chris walks 5 km due south and then 8 km due east.
 How far is Chris from his starting point?

6 A rectangle is 2 m long. Its diagonal is 3 m long.
 Work out the width of the rectangle, to the nearest centimetre.

7 The diagonal length of a laptop computer screen is advertised as 40 cm.
 The width of the screen is 23 cm.
 Work out the length of the laptop computer screen.
 Give your answer to the nearest whole centimetre.

8 The length of a rectangle is 50 cm and its diagonal is 51 cm.
 Work out the area of the rectangle, to the nearest square centimetre.

9 The diagram shows a triangle inscribed in a circle with centre O.
 The lengths of the shorter sides of the triangle are 6 cm and 8 cm.
 Work out the area of the circle.
 Use π = 3.14.

 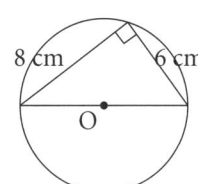

8 Constructions and Pythagoras' theorem

9 Expressions and formulae

Exercise 9.1 Simplifying algebraic expressions

1 Simplify each expression.
   a $a^3 \times a^4$
   b $b^5 \times b^5$
   c $c^7 \times c^8$
   d $d^8 \times d^2$
   e $e^4 \times e^2$
   f $f \times f^3$
   g $g^8 \div g^4$
   h $h^6 \div h^2$
   i $i^{10} \div i^5$
   j $j^8 \div j^2$
   k $k^8 \div k^7$
   l $l^8 \div l$

2 Simplify each expression.
   a $2a^2 \times 2a^2$ b $4b^4 \times 4b^4$
   c $6c^6 \times 6c^6$ d $8d^3 \times 8d^3$
   e $10e^6 \times e^5$ f $f^9 \times 12f$
   g $16g^{12} \div 2g^4$ h $9h^9 \div 3h^3$
   i $10x^4 \div 5x$ j $\dfrac{10x^{10}}{2x^2}$
   k $\dfrac{5x^5}{x}$ l $\dfrac{11x^{11}}{x^{10}}$

3 Which is the correct answer, A, B, C or D?
   a Simplify $3a^3 \times 4a^2$.   A $7a^5$ B $12a^5$ C $7a^6$ D $12a^6$
   b Simplify $4b^3 \times 5b$.   A $20b^4$ B $20b^3$ C $9b^4$ D $9b^3$
   c Simplify $15c^6 \div 5c^3$.   A $3c^3$ B $10c^2$ C $3c^2$ D $10c^3$
   d Simplify $\dfrac{9d^5}{3d}$.   A $3d^5$ B $6d^5$ C $6d^4$ D $3d^4$

 4 Look at these algebra cards.

$x^6 \times 3x^3$

$9x^{12} \div x^9$

$2x \times 3x^5$

$3x^3 \times 2x^3$

$9x^9 \div 3x^3$

$12x^{12} \div 4x^3$

$6x^6 \times x^3$

   a Sort the cards into two groups.
     Explain how you decided to sort the groups.
   b Which card does not fit into either of the groups?
     Explain why you chose this card.

Exercise 9.2 Constructing algebraic expressions

1 Oditi thinks of a number, n.

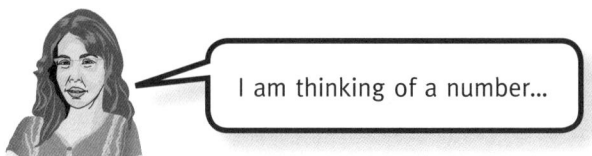

I am thinking of a number…

Write an expression, in terms of n, for the number Oditi gets when she:
a adds 1 to the number
b subtracts 10 from the number
c multiplies the number by 100
d divides the number by 1000
e multiplies the number by 2 then adds 3
f divides the number by 4 then subtracts 5
g multiplies the number by 6 then subtracts 7
h divides the number by 8 then adds 9
i divides 1 by the number then subtracts 1
j divides 10 by double the number
k adds 20 to the number then multiplies the result by 3
l subtracts 3 from the number then multiplies the result by 20.

2 Write an expression, in terms of x, for the perimeter of each shape.
Write each expression in its simplest form.

a 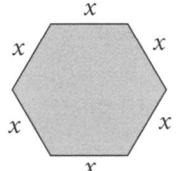   b 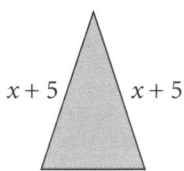   c 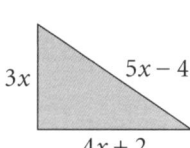   d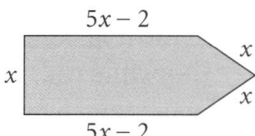

3 Write an expression for the area of each shape.
Write each expression in its simplest form.

a 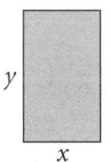   b 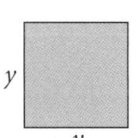   c 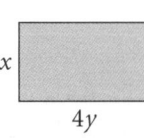   d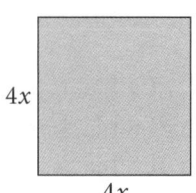

4 Write an expression for:
  i the perimeter   ii the area of each rectangle.
Write each answer in its simplest form.
Expand brackets where necessary.

a 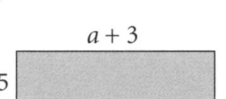   b    c 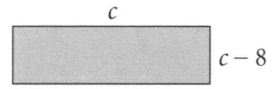   d

9 Expressions and formulae   41

5 Jake and Razi have four different rods.
The length of each grey rod is $a + 2$.
The length of each black rod is $a + 3$.
The length of each white rod is $2a + 2$.
The length of each striped rod is $3a + 1$.

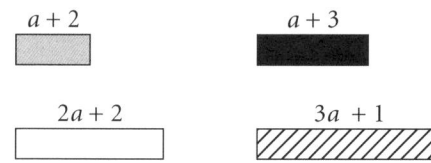

Look at the lengths of the rods.

Jake shows Razi that the total length of two black rods and four striped rods is the same as the total length of four white rods and two striped rods, like this.

> 2 black + 4 striped   4 white + 2 striped
> $= 2(a + 3) + 4(3a + 1)$ $= 4(2a + 2) + 2(3a + 1)$
> $= 2a + 6 + 12a + 4$ $= 8a + 8 + 6a + 2$
> $= 14a + 10$ $= 14a + 10$

a Show that:
  i   the total length of 2 black rods and 2 striped rods is the same as the total length of 4 white rods
  ii the total length of 3 black rods and 3 striped rods is the same as the total length of 6 white rods
  iii the total length of 5 black rods and 5 striped rods is the same as the total length of 10 white rods.

b What do your answers to part **a** tell you about the connection between the number of black and striped rods and the number of white rods?

c Show that:
  i   the total length of 4 black rods and 2 white rods is the same as the total length of 8 grey rods
  ii the total length of 6 black rods and 3 white rods is the same as the total length of 12 grey rods
  iii the total length of 8 black rods and 4 white rods is the same as the total length of 16 grey rods.

d What do your answers to part **c** tell you about the connection between the number of black and white rods and the number of grey rods?

Exercise 9.3 Substituting into expressions

1 Work out the value of each expression when $a = 2$, $b = -3$, $c = 4$ and $d = -5$.
   a $b + d$
   b $a + 2b$
   c $2d - b$
   d $a - c$
   e $4b + 2a$
   f $3d - 6b$
   g $bd - 10$
   h $cd^2 + ab$
   i $\frac{d}{2} - a$
   j $20 - a^3$
   k $ab + cd$
   l $\frac{bc}{a} + d$

2 Work out the value of each expression when $w = 3$, $x = 2$, $y = -4$ and $z = -2$.
   a $3(w + x)$
   b $x(2w - y)$
   c $z(2w - y)$
   d $w - z^3$
   e $x^2 + z^2$
   f $(2z)^3$
   g $\frac{x}{2} - \frac{y}{4}$
   h $\frac{wx}{z} + y$
   i $2(x^3 - z^2)$
   j $20 - 2w^2$
   k $w + z(3x - 2y)$
   l $3(w + x) - 5(w - x)$

3 This is part of Sasha's homework.

> *Question* Use a counter-example to show that the statement $3x^2 = (3x)^2$ is *not* always true.
>
> *Answer* Let $x = 3$, so $3x^2 = 3 \times 3^2 = 2 \times 9 = 27$ and $(3x)^2 = (3 \times 3)^2 = 9^2 = 81$
>
> $27 \neq 81$, so $3x^2 \neq (3x)^2$

Use a counter-example to show that each of these statements is *not* always true.
   a $10a^2 = (10a)^2$
   b $(2b)^3 = 2b^3$
   c $3c - 3d = 3(d - c)$

◆ Exercise 9.4 Deriving and using formulae

1. **a** Write a formula for the number of hours, H, in any number of days, D.
   b Use your formula in part **a** to work out the value of H when $D = 10$.
   c Rearrange your formula in part **a** to make D the subject.
   d Use you formula in part **c** to work out the value of D when $H = 480$.

2. Use the formula $D = ST$ to work out the value of:
   a D when $S = 50$ and $T = 3$
   b D when $S = 120$ and $T = 1.5$
   c S when $D = 100$ and $T = 5$
   d T when $D = 22$ and $S = 4$.

   > In question 2 parts **c** and **d**, start by changing the subject of the formula.

3. Use the formula $F = I + ae$ to work out the value of:
   a F when $I = 5$, $a = 10$ and $e = 2$
   b F when $I = 0$, $a = 9$ and $e = 6$
   c I when $F = 100$, $a = 4$ and $e = 15$
   d I when $F = 36$, $a = 2$ and $e = 7.5$
   e e when $F = 50$, $I = 10$ and $a = 8$
   f a when $F = 48$, $I = 34$ and $e = 2$.

4. Stanley is d years old. Polly is 3 years <u>older</u> than Stanley.
   a Write an expression for Polly's age in terms of d.
   b Write a formula for the total age, T, of Stanley and Polly.
   c Use your formula in part **b** to work out the value of T when $d = 8$.
   d Rearrange your formula in part **c** to make d the subject.
   e Use your formula in part **d** to work out the value of d when $T = 27$.

5. Kimma buys and sells furniture. She uses the formula in the box work to out the percentage profit she makes.
   Work out the percentage profit that Kimma makes on each piece of furniture.

   > Percentage profit = $\dfrac{\text{selling price} - \text{cost price}}{\text{cost price}} \times 100$

   a Cost price = \$28, selling price = \$42
   b Cost price = \$150, selling price = \$162
   c Cost price = \$35, selling price = \$73.50

6. In many countries, the distance of a horse race is measured in furlongs (F) and yards (Y).
   A formula to convert furlongs and yards into metres (m) is shown in the box.
   Work out the distance, in metres, of each horse race below.
   Give each answer correct to the nearest metre.

   > $m = \dfrac{220F + Y}{1.09}$ where: m is the number of metres
   > F is the number of furlongs
   > Y is the number of yards.

   a 2 furlongs and 50 yards
   b 6 furlongs and 100 yards
   c 5 furlongs and 75 yards
   d 8 furlongs

7. Anders knows this relationship between temperatures in degrees Fahrenheit (°F) and temperatures in degrees Celsius (°C).

   > $F = 1.8C + 32$ where: F is the temperature in degrees Fahrenheit (°F)
   > C is the temperature in degrees Celsius (°C).

   > I think that a temperature of 20 °C is higher than 65 °F.

   Is Anders correct?
   Show how you worked out your answer.

Exercise 9.5 Factorising

1. Copy and complete each factorisation.
   a. $6a + 24 = 6(a + \square)$
   b. $9c - 15 = 3(3c - \square)$
   c. $4ef + 16f = 4f(e + \square)$
   d. $7g^2 + g = g(7g + \square)$
   e. $8 - 12j = 4(\square - \square)$
   f. $7m^2 - 4m = m(\square - \square)$

2. Factorise each expression.
   a. $5z + 15$
   b. $2y - 14$
   c. $20x + 4$
   d. $9w - 3$
   e. $6v + 8$
   f. $14u - 21$
   g. $12 - 6u$
   h. $14 + 21v$
   i. $12 - 15w$
   j. $16 + 24x$
   k. $8 + 14y$
   l. $14 - 35z$

3. Factorise each expression.
   a. $7m^2 + m$
   b. $5a^2 - 15a$
   c. $t^2 + 9t$
   d. $8h - 4h^2$
   e. $3s + 12s^2$
   f. $12y - 16y^2$
   g. $16e - 8i$
   h. $15e + 6i$
   i. $14ei - 7e$
   j. $12a + 8ab$
   k. $21g + 15gh$
   l. $30w - 15tw$

4. Copy and complete each factorisation.
   a. $2a + 4h + 8 = 2(a + 2h + \square)$
   b. $5b - 25 + 5j = 5(b - \square + j)$
   c. $12tu + 16u - 20 = 4(3tu + \square - 5)$
   d. $3e^2 + 4e + ef = e(3e + \square + \square)$
   e. $7k - k^2 - ak = k(\square - \square - \square)$
   f. $6n^2 - 9n + 3mn = 3n(\square - \square + \square)$

5. Read what Tanesha says.

   When I expand $5(3x - 2) - 5(2 + x)$ then collect like terms and finally factorise the result, I get the expression $20(x - 1)$.

   Show that Tanesha is wrong.
   Explain the mistake that she has made.

Exercise 9.6 Adding and subtracting algebraic fractions

1 Simplify each expression.

> In this exercise, give each answer as a fraction in its simplest form and as a mixed number when appropriate.

a $\dfrac{x}{3} + \dfrac{x}{3}$

b $\dfrac{x}{5} + \dfrac{2x}{5}$

c $\dfrac{x}{6} + \dfrac{x}{6}$

d $\dfrac{5x}{7} - \dfrac{x}{7}$

e $\dfrac{7x}{8} - \dfrac{x}{8}$

f $\dfrac{7x}{10} - \dfrac{3x}{10}$

g $\dfrac{y}{3} + \dfrac{y}{6}$

h $\dfrac{2y}{3} + \dfrac{7y}{9}$

i $\dfrac{2y}{3} + \dfrac{11y}{18}$

j $\dfrac{y}{3} - \dfrac{y}{9}$

k $\dfrac{3y}{4} - \dfrac{y}{24}$

l $\dfrac{5y}{8} - \dfrac{5y}{16}$

2 Simplify each expression.

a $\dfrac{x}{2} + \dfrac{y}{2}$ b $\dfrac{x}{3} + \dfrac{y}{6}$ c $\dfrac{3x}{4} + \dfrac{y}{12}$

d $\dfrac{5x}{6} - \dfrac{y}{18}$ e $\dfrac{7x}{12} - \dfrac{2y}{3}$ f $\dfrac{7x}{18} - \dfrac{5y}{6}$

g $\dfrac{a}{5} + \dfrac{b}{4}$ h $\dfrac{3a}{4} + \dfrac{b}{7}$ i $\dfrac{5a}{9} + \dfrac{5b}{6}$

j $\dfrac{a}{7} - \dfrac{b}{5}$ k $\dfrac{5a}{8} - \dfrac{b}{12}$ l $\dfrac{2a}{7} - \dfrac{5b}{6}$

3 Here are some algebraic fraction cards.

A $\dfrac{9x}{10} - \dfrac{13x}{20}$ B $\dfrac{x}{6} + \dfrac{x}{3}$ C $\dfrac{2x}{7} + \dfrac{3x}{14}$

D $\dfrac{11x}{18} - \dfrac{13x}{36}$ E $\dfrac{11x}{15} - \dfrac{2x}{5}$ F $\dfrac{x}{12} + \dfrac{x}{6}$

a Sort the cards into two groups.
   Explain your reasons for sorting the cards.
b Which card does not fit into either of the groups?
   Explain why you chose this card.
c Explain how you can use normal fractions rather than algebraic fractions to work out the answers to part a.

Exercise 9.7 Expanding the product of two linear expressions

1 Expand and simplify each expression.
   a $(x + 5)(x + 2)$
   b $(x + 6)(x + 1)$
   c $(x + 4)(x - 2)$
   d $(x - 6)(x + 3)$
   e $(x - 3)(x - 3)$
   f $(x - 5)(x - 8)$
   g $(x + 5)(x + 10)$
   h $(x - 5)(x + 10)$
   i $(x - 5)(x - 10)$

2 Which answer is correct, **A**, **B** or **C**?
   a $(w + 7)(w + 8) =$ **A** $w^2 + 15w + 15$ **B** $w^2 + 15w + 56$ **C** $w^2 + w + 56$
   b $(x + 5)(x - 3) =$ **A** $x^2 + 2x - 15$ **B** $x^2 - 8x - 2$ **C** $x^2 + 8x - 15$
   c $(y - 6)(y + 4) =$ **A** $y^2 - 10y - 2$ **B** $y^2 - 2y - 2$ **C** $y^2 - 2y - 24$
   d $(z - 3)(z - 5) =$ **A** $z^2 - 2z + 8$ **B** $z^2 + 8z - 15$ **C** $z^2 - 8z + 15$

3 Expand and simplify each expression.
   a $(a + 2)^2$
   b $(b + 4)^2$
   c $(c + 1)^2$
   d $(d - 3)^2$
   e $(e - 5)^2$
   f $(f - 1)^2$

4 a Expand and simplify each expression.
     i $(a - 1)(a + 1)$ ii $(a - 4)(a + 4)$ iii $(a + 9)(a - 9)$
  b What do you notice about your answers in part **a**?
  c Write down the simplified expansion of $(a - 8)(a + 8)$.
  d Write down the simplified expansion of $(a + b)(a - b)$.

10 Processing and presenting data

◆ Exercise 10.1 Calculating statistics

1. These are the numbers of people who were late for work during a period of 24 days.

   1 5 0 2 0 1 3 6 1 0 0 0
   2 0 2 4 0 4 2 1 1 0 6 0

   a Find the modal number of people late.
   b Work out the median number of people late.
   c Work out the mean number of people late per day.

2. This bar chart shows the number of goals scored by a football team in 20 matches.

   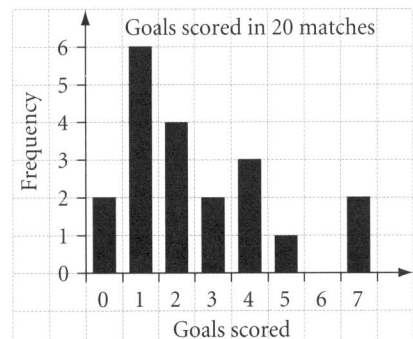

   a Find the modal number of goals.
   b Work out the median number of goals.
   c Work out the mean number of goals per match.
   d In the next match the team scored five goals.
   Work out the new value of:
   i the mode **ii** the median **iii** the mean.

3. This graph shows the times it took for Greg to travel to work on 35 different days.

   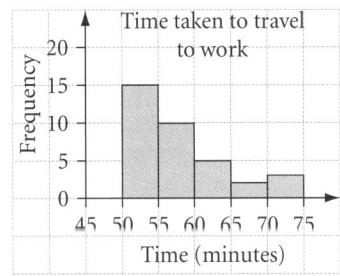

   a Find the modal class.
   b What can you say about the median time it took for Greg to travel to work?

4 Forty students were given five simple tasks to do.
This table shows the results.

Tasks completed	0	1	2	3	4	5
Frequency	1	3	3	4	10	19

  a Show that the mode is greater than the median.
  b Show that the median is greater than the mean.

5 The mean mass of five boys is 10.5 kg. The mean mass of three girls is 9.5 kg.
Work out the mean mass of the eight young children.

6 A group of students worked on a computer puzzle.
This table shows the times it took them to complete it.

Time (seconds)	16–20	21–25	26–30	31–35	36–40
Boys	3	12	25	28	14
Girls	15	21	17	7	15

Find the modal class for:
  a the boys   **b** the girls   **c** the whole group.

◆ Exercise 10.2 Using statistics

1. Alicia is doing a survey on the number of matches in a box.

   The label on a box says: 'Average contents 40 matches'.

   Alicia counts the matches in ten boxes.
   Here are the numbers she finds.
   42 39 41 41 41 37 40 41 39 42

   a Is the statement on the box correct?
   Give a reason for your answer.

   b Should Alicia complain?

2. These are the midday temperatures, in degrees Celsius (°C), in a town for one week.
   16 18 24 28 26 19 17
   Jake and Oditi are comparing the temperature.
   Read what they say.

    The average temperature is less than 20 °C.

    The average temperature is more than 20 °C.

   Explain how they could both be correct.

3. This table shows some students' marks in an exam.

Marks	26–30	31–35	36–40	41–45	46–50
Boys	6	12	17	15	8
Girls	0	3	8	9	7

   a Use an appropriate average to compare the boys' marks with the girls' marks.
   b What can you say about the spread of the boys' marks and the girls' marks?

4. During the season, a website gave these attendance figures for some football teams' home games.

Team	Manchester United	AC Milan	Barcelona
Total attendance	1 055 127	718 972	1 140 240
Average attendance	75 366	51 355	81 445

   a Which average has been used?
   b Work out how many games each team had played.
   c Borussia Dortmund had the largest attendance in the German Bundesliga.
   They had an average attendance of 80 460 from 13 games.
   What was the total attendance?

5 Here are the ages of the people in two different clubs.
Music Club: 28 34 42 29 51 39 36 48 27 45 30 33 39 28 33 37
Book Club: 38 44 53 49 47 52 48 43 51 39 46

a On average, which club has the older members?
Give a reason for your answer.

b Which club has more variation in ages?
Give a reason for your answer.

6 This table shows the ages of the finishers in the 2011 New York Marathon.

Age	18–24	25–29	30–34	35–39	40–44	45–49	50–54	55–64	65–74	75–84	Total
Men	825	2616	3968	4900	5928	4588	3768	2896	525	44	30 058
Women	691	2867	3122	2880	3072	2135	1468	902	115	13	17 265

On average, who were older, the men or the women?
Give a reason for your answer.

> The oldest competitor was Joy Johnson, age 84. Her time was 7 hours 45 minutes.

11 Percentages

◆ Exercise 11.1 Using mental methods

> Do not use a calculator in this exercise.

1. 30% of a sum of money is $234.
   Use this fact to work out:
   a. 60%
   b. 90%
   c. 15%
   d. 3%
   of the same amount.

2. a. Describe how to find 35% of a number, without using a calculator.
   b. Find 35% of:
      i. 44 kg
      ii. 280 m
      iii. $88.

3. Work out:
   a. 51% of 430
   b. 98% of 2700
   c. 9% of 640
   d. 2.5% of 12 800.

4. 63% of 648 = 408.24

   Use this fact to find:
   a. 63% of 324 kg
   b. 21% of $648
   c. 126% of 648 m
   d. 6.3% of 648 litres.

5. Copy and complete this table.

Amount	164	328	82	16.4	
65% of the amount	106.6				21.32

6. a. One is different from the other three. Which one?
      A. 23% of 846
      B. 46% of 423
      C. 69% of 272
      D. 92% of 211.5
   b. Give a reason for your answer.

7. 32% of 1600 = 512

   Use this fact to work out:
   a. 64% of 1600
   b. 96% of 1600
   c. 132% of 1600
   d. 232% of 1600.

8. Put these in order of size, smallest first.
   A. 20% of 5600
   B. 10% of 12 000
   C. 5% of 20 000
   D. 2% of 49 900

Exercise 11.2 Comparing different quantities

1. In an English exam Zalika scored 53 out of 70.
   In a science exam she scored 37 out of 45.

    I did better in the English exam than in the science.

   Use percentages to check whether Zalika is correct.

2. In a group of 420 young people, 37 wear glasses.
   In a group of 1570 older people, 423 wear glasses.
   Compare the percentages that wear glasses in each group.

3. Rovers and United are two football teams.
   Rovers won 14 matches, drew 7 and lost 10.
   United won 8 matches, drew 2 and lost 3.
   a Find the percentage of matches that each team won.
   b Which team has the better record for winning matches?

4. In 2012 there was an election for the president of France.
   The two candidates were Monsieur Hollande and Monsieur Sarkozy.
   These are the numbers of votes cast in two regions of France.

Candidate	M Hollande	M Sarkozy
Paris	560 459	447 499
Corsica	70 148	88 799

   Find the percentage of the regional vote for M Hollande in:
   a Paris   b Corsica.

5. In a games lesson at school, some children chose whether to play tennis or badminton.

	Boys	Girls	Total
Tennis	23	41	64
Badminton	52	25	77
Total	75	66	141

   a Calculate the percentage of the tennis players who were:
      i boys   ii girls.
   b Compare the percentages of the badminton players who were boys and girls.
   c
    31% of the boys chose tennis.

   Is Razi correct?
   Give a reason for your answer.

   d
    In this group, girls are more likely than boys to choose tennis.

   Is Mia correct?
   Give a reason for your answer.

◆ Exercise 11.3 Percentage changes

1. These are the prices of three items of furniture in Jean-Luc's shop.

   Carpet $720   Table $460   Chair $240

   In a special sale, Jean-Luc reduced all the prices by $100.
   Find the percentage reduction in each price.

2. The population of a town was 23 000.
   After some new houses were built, the population increased to 24 500.
   Work out the percentage increase in population.

3. Darwin's best time for running 5000 metres is 16 minutes.
   He wants to run it in 15 minutes 30 seconds.
   What percentage reduction in time is this?

4. The table shows Julika's mass in four months of the same year.

Month	January	April	July	October
Mass (kg)	51.2	54.6	52.7	48.9

   Calculate the percentage change in Julika's mass:
   a. from January to April
   b. from April to October
   c. from July to October.

5. On 1 June, a plant was 20 cm high.
   It grew 2 cm every week.
   Find the percentage increase when the height changed from:
   a. 20 cm to 22 cm
   b. 22 cm to 24 cm
   c. 24 cm to 26 cm
   d. 28 cm to 30 cm

6. In 1900, the population of a country was 12.8 million.
   In 2000, the population was 29.4 million.
   a. Work out the percentage increase in population from 1900 to 2000.
   b. If the percentage increase is the same in the next 100 years, estimate the population in 2100.

7. a. The speed of a car increased from 80 km/h to 90 km/h.
      Calculate the percentage increase.
   b. The speed of a car decreased from 90 km/h to 80 km/h.
      Calculate the percentage decrease.
   c. A car was travelling at 70 km/h.
      The speed increased by 7%.
      Calculate the new speed.

8.
   A: Two for the price of one!

   B: Buy two, get one free!

   C: Buy one, get the second half price!

   a. Find the percentage reduction for each of these special offers.
   b. Which is the best offer?

Exercise 11.4 Practical examples

1. Ferdinand bought four items on the internet. Two weeks later, he sold them.
   The table shows what he paid for them (cost price) and what he sold them for (selling price).

Item	Radio	Television	Computer	Jewellery
Cost price (dollars)	40	360	520	275
Selling price (dollars)	52	400	460	345

   Calculate the percentage profit or loss for each item.

2. The cost of a mathematics textbook is 25 dollars.
   A school gets a 15% discount because it buys 60 books.
   Calculate the total reduction in price.

3. A man earns $65 000.
   He pays 18% of that in tax.
   a Calculate how much he has left, after paying the tax.
   b He invests $4500 and earns 6% interest per annum.
      Calculate the interest after one year.
   c He takes out a loan to buy a car.
      The price of the car is $24 750.
      He pays $25 740 altogether.
      What is the percentage interest?

4. A shopkeeper bought 24 bottles of fruit juice for $63 dollars.
   She sold them for $2.95 each.
   Calculate her percentage profit or loss.

5. A sales tax of 9% is added to the price of the items sold in a shop.
   The prices of three items, before tax is added, are shown in the box.
   Calculate the price of each item after tax has been added.

   > Hockey stick $75
   > Football boots $92
   > Track suit $129

6. A man takes a loan of $45 000.
   The interest is 3%.
   He pays the loan with 36 equal payments.
   How much is each payment?

7. Tax is paid on meals in a restaurant.
   The price of a meal was $57.23. This <u>includes</u> tax of $8.73.
   What is the percentage tax?

   > Be careful! What is the tax a percentage of?

8. Income tax is calculated like this.

   > *First $20 000   no tax*
   > *$20 000 to $40 000   15%*
   > *Over $40 000   25%*
   > *Example: If you earn $25 000, you pay 15% of ($25 000 - $20 000) = $750*
   > *On $45 000, you pay 15% of ($40 000 - $20 000) + 25% of ($45 000 - £40 000)*
   >   *= $3000 + $1250 = $4250*

   Work out the income tax paid by someone who earns:
   a $19 000   b $29 000   c $49 000.

12 Tessellations, transformations and loci

✦ Exercise 12.1 Tessellating shapes

1 Show how each of these quadrilaterals and triangles will tessellate.
   Draw a tessellation of each shape on squared paper.
   Draw at least five of each shape to show how it tessellates.

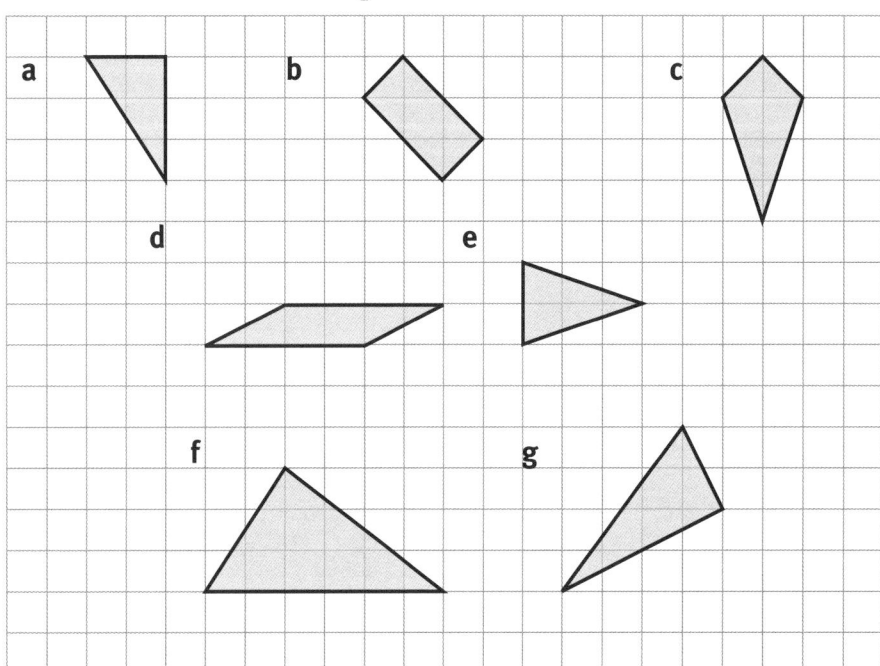

Use tracing paper for shape **g**.

2 Explain why any square will tessellate.
  Show all your working and include diagrams in your explanation.

3 Read what Ahmad says.

> A regular 10-sided shape is called a decagon. A decagon will not tessellate.

Explain why Ahmad is correct.
Show all your working in your explanation.

Exercise 12.2 Solving transformation problems

1 The diagram shows shape A on a coordinate grid.
  Copy the grid, then draw the image of shape A after each translation.

  a $\begin{pmatrix} 2 \\ 1 \end{pmatrix}$ b $\begin{pmatrix} 1 \\ -2 \end{pmatrix}$

  c $\begin{pmatrix} -3 \\ 2 \end{pmatrix}$ d $\begin{pmatrix} -2 \\ -1 \end{pmatrix}$

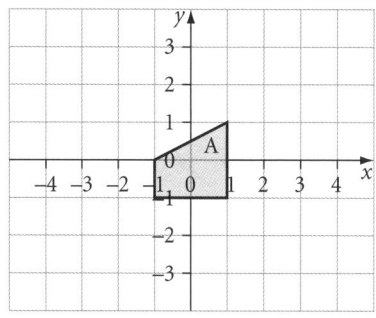

2 The diagram shows triangle B on a coordinate grid.
  Copy the grid.
  Draw the image of triangle B after a reflection in the line:
  a $x = 2$
  b $x = 3.5$
  c $y = 3$.

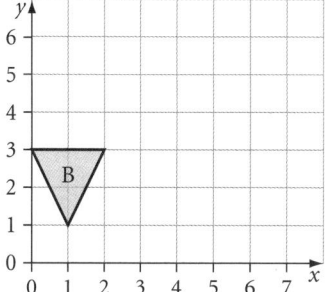

3 The diagram shows shape C on a coordinate grid.
  Copy the grid.
  Draw the image of shape C after a rotation:
  a 90° clockwise about the point (5, 3)
  b 90° anticlockwise about the point (2, 3)
  c 180° about the point (3, 2)
  d 180° about the point (4, 5).

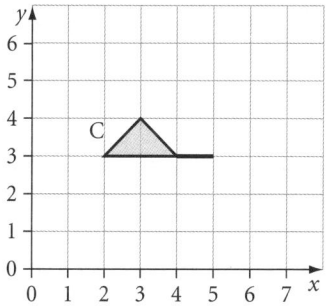

4 Copy this grid, with the shape drawn on it.
  a Reflect the triangle in the line $x = 4$.
  b Reflect the triangle in the line $y = 3$.

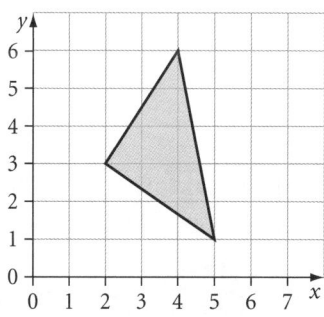

12 Tessellations, transformations and loci

5 The diagram shows shape P on a coordinate grid.
   One corner of shape P is marked with a cross.
   Xavier rotates object shape P through 90° clockwise about the
   point (−2, 1) and labels the image shape Q.
   Then he translates object shape P, using the column vector $\begin{pmatrix} -2 \\ -4 \end{pmatrix}$,
   and labels the image shape R.
   Read what Xavier says.

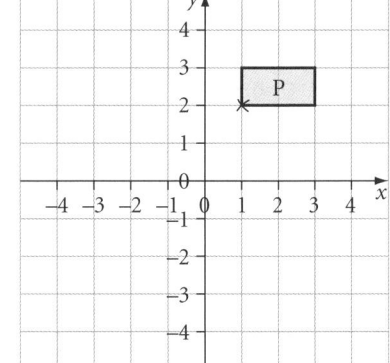

The crosses on shapes Q and R have exactly the same coordinates.

Show that Xavier is correct.

6 The diagram shows shape ABCD on a coordinate grid.
   a Write down the coordinates of the points A, B, C and D.
   The diagram also shows the line with equation $y = x$.
   Copy the grid.
   b Reflect shape ABCD in the line $y = x$ and label the image A'B'C'D'.
   c Write down the coordinates of the points A', B', C' and D'.
   d Compare your answers to parts **a** and **c**. What do you notice
      about the coordinates of ABCD and its image A'B'C'D'?

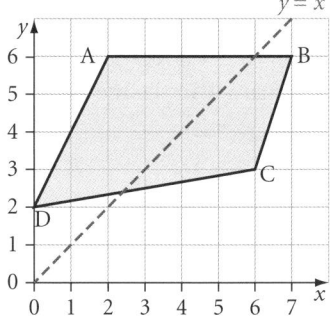

7 Dakarai wrote this question in his homework book.

   On the coordinate grid draw these transformations.
     a A reflection of the shape in the line $y = 3$
     b A rotation of the shape 90° anticlockwise about the point (3, 3).

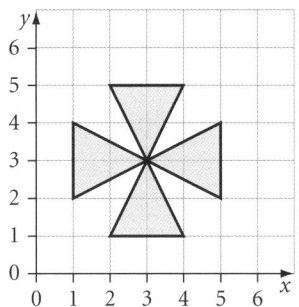

Dakarai forgot to do his homework, so he gave in his book without answering the question.
Read what Dakarai says when the teacher gives him the book back.

I have been given 100%!

Explain how this is possible.

12 Tessellations, transformations and loci

Exercise 12.3 Transforming shapes

1. The diagram shows triangle A on a coordinate grid. Copy the grid.
   On your diagram, draw the image of A after each combination of transformations.

   a A reflection in the y-axis followed by the translation $\begin{pmatrix} 2 \\ 1 \end{pmatrix}$

   b A rotation of 180°, centre $(-2, -2)$, followed by a reflection in the x-axis

   c A translation $\begin{pmatrix} -2 \\ 6 \end{pmatrix}$, followed by a rotation of 90° anticlockwise, centre $(-3, 5)$

   d A translation $\begin{pmatrix} 6 \\ 7 \end{pmatrix}$, followed by a reflection in the line $x = 4$

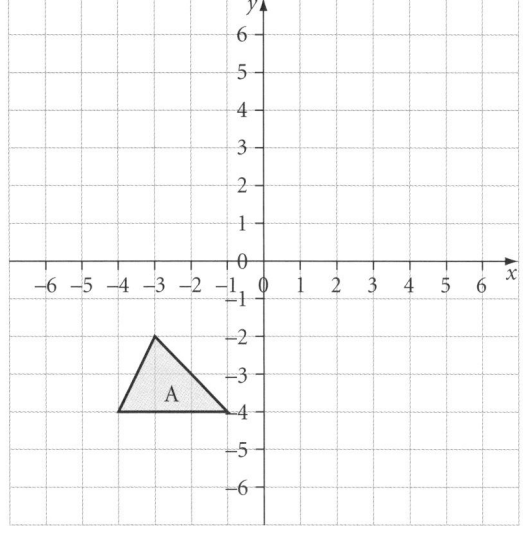

2. The diagram shows shapes G, H, I, J, K, L, M and N.
   Describe the reflection that transforms:
   a shape G to shape H
   b shape G to shape J
   c shape H to shape I
   d shape J to shape K
   e shape L to shape K.
   Describe the rotation that transforms:
   f shape J to shape M
   g shape J to shape H
   h shape N to shape G.

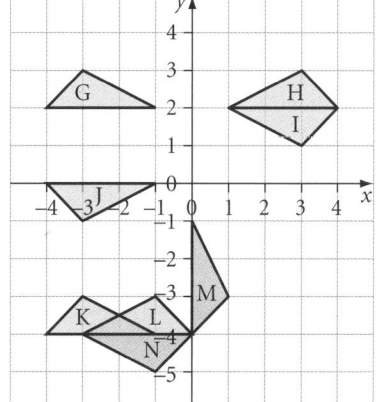

3. The diagram shows shapes A, B, C, D, E, F and G on a coordinate grid.
   a Describe the single transformation that transforms:
   i shape A to shape C
   ii shape A to shape D
   iii shape E to shape G
   iv shape E to shape F.
   b Describe a combined transformation that transforms:
   i shape C to shape F
   ii shape D to shape B.

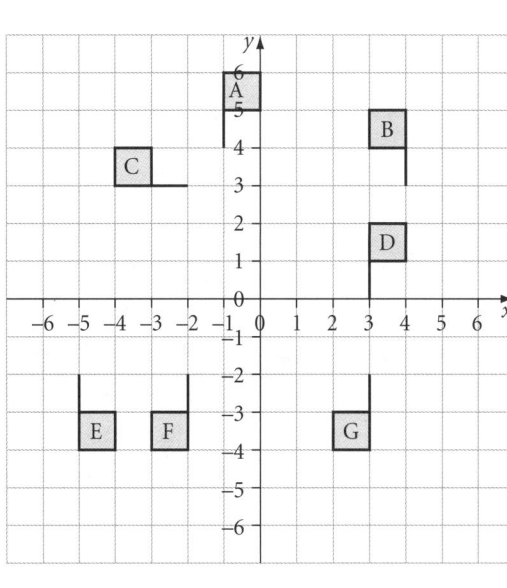

◆ Exercise 12.4　Enlarging shapes

1. The diagram shows a triangle on a coordinate grid.
   Copy the grid.
   a Draw an enlargement of the triangle with scale factor 2, centre (3, 1).
   b Draw an enlargement of the triangle with scale factor 3, centre (1, 0).

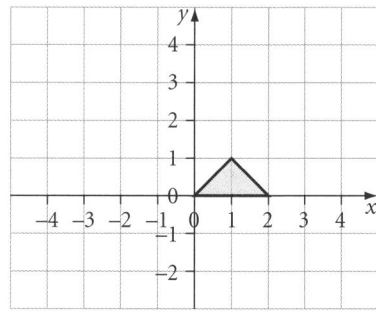

2. The diagram shows three triangles, A, B and C, on a coordinate grid.
   a Triangle B is an enlargement of triangle A. Describe the enlargement.
   b Triangle C is an enlargement of triangle A. Describe the enlargement.

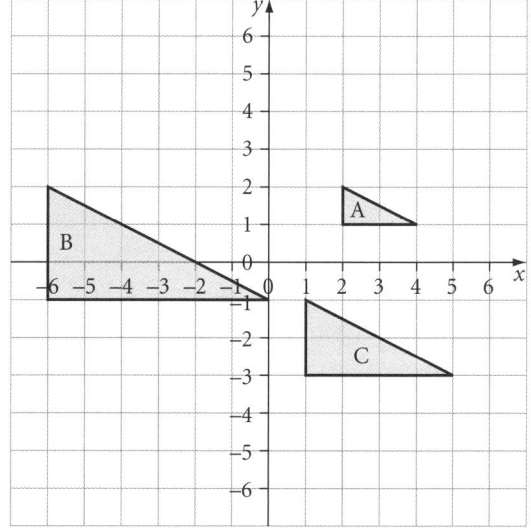

3. The vertices of rectangle P are at (0, −2), (−6, −2), (−6, 1) and (0, 1).
   The vertices of rectangle Q are at (4, 0), (2, 0), (2, 1) and (4, 1).
   Rectangle P is an enlargement of rectangle Q.
   Describe the enlargement.

4. Anders draws a square with vertices at (−1, −1), (−3, −1), (−3, 1) and (−1, 1).
   He enlarges the shape, using a scale factor of 2, centre (0, 0).

   If I multiply the coordinates of each vertex of the square by 2, it will work out that the coordinates of the enlarged square are at (−2, −2), (−6, −2), (−6, 2) and (−2, 2).

   a Show, by drawing, that in this case Anders is correct.

   This means that for an enlargement of any square, with a scale factor of 2 and any centre of enlargement, I can multiply the coordinates of each vertex by 2 to work out the coordinates of the enlarged square.

   b Use a counter-example to show that this is not true.
      (Remember that a counter-example is just one example that shows a statement is not true.)

Exercise 12.5 Drawing a locus

1. On a sheet of plain paper, draw a point and label it A.
   Draw the locus of points that are exactly 4.5 cm from point A.

2. Draw a segment of a straight horizontal line.
   Draw the locus of points that are exactly 3 cm from the line.

3. Draw a line segment PQ, 6 cm long.
   Draw the locus of points that are exactly 4 cm from PQ.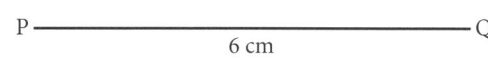

 4. A goat is tied by a rope to a post in the centre of a large field.
   The rope is 6 m long.
   Draw the locus of points that the goat can reach when the rope is tight.
   Use a scale of 1 cm to 2 m.

 5. Tanesha has a coin of radius 1.5 cm.
   She rolls the coin around the outside of a rectangular box,
   so that it is always touching the sides of the box.
   The box is 6 cm wide by 8 cm long.
   Draw the locus of C, the centre of the coin.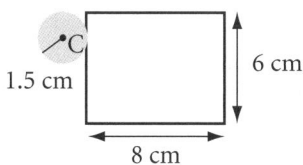

 6. Draw these shapes on centimetre-squared paper.
   For each shape, draw the locus of points that are 1 cm from the lines of the shape.

   a   b   c

 7. The diagram shows a rectangular field WXYZ.
   There is a fence around the perimeter of the field.
   Don the donkey is tied by a rope to corner Z of the field.
   When the rope is tight, Don can just reach corner Y.
   Copy the diagram.
   a Draw the locus of points that Don can reach when the rope is tight.
   b Shade the region that Don cannot reach.

 8. The diagram shows two radio transmitters, W and X,
   160 km apart.
   Transmitter W has a range of 100 km.
   Transmitter X has a range of 80 km.
   Copy the diagram. Use a scale of 1 cm to 20 km.

   W •━━━━━━━━━━━━━━━━━━• X
              160 km

   a Draw the locus of points that are exactly 100 km from W.
   b Draw the locus of points that are exactly 80 km from X.
   c Shade the region in where both transmitters are in range.

12 Tessellations, transformations and loci

13 Equations and inequalities

Exercise 13.1 Solving linear equations

1. Solve these equations.
   a. $3g - 5 = 31$
   b. $3g - 5 = -20$
   c. $-3g - 5 = 25$
   d. $-5 + 3g = 16$

2. Solve these equations.
   a. $7 + 4p = 28$
   b. $7(4 + p) = 28$
   c. $7 + 4p = 28 + p$
   d. $7 + 4p = 2p + 8$

3. Solve these equations. Write the solutions as fractions.
   a. $7y + 13 = 31$
   b. $6(y - 7) = 25$
   c. $15 = 40 - 8y$
   d. $5y - 12 = 40 - 4y$

4. Solve these equations.
   a. $5x + 40 = 0$
   b. $0 = 17(15 + 5x)$
   c. $4x + 20 = x - 17$
   d. $5(x + 5) + 3(x - 2) = 3$

5. Here is an equation.

   $5(x + 3) = 10x - 20$

   a. Solve it by first multiplying out the brackets.
   b. Solve it by first dividing by 5.

6. Look at this equation.

   $8(x - 4) + 4(5 - x) = 0$

   a. Solve the equation by first multiplying out the two brackets.
   b. Solve the equation by first dividing by 4.

7. Solve these equations.
   a. $13 - 2x = 5$
   b. $13 - 2(x + 7) = 5$
   c. $13 - 2(x - 7) = 5$

8. Shen is solving an equation.
   There is a mistake in the second line of his solution.
   a. Correct the mistake.
   b. Solve the equation.

   $5(x + 6) = 2(30 - x)$
   $\rightarrow 5x + 11 = 60 - x$

9. Look at this equation.

   $4(x - 2) = 40 - 2x$

   Solve it in two different ways.

Exercise 13.2 Solving problems

1. Two numbers are n and $2(n+3)$.
   a The sum of the numbers is 90.
      Write down an equation to show this.
   b Solve the equation.
   c Find the two numbers.

2. In the algebra wall, each number or expression is the sum of the two below it.
   a Write expressions for the numbers in the two empty cells.
   b The number in the top cell is 144.
      Write an equation to show this.
   c Solve the equation.

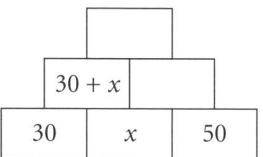

3. The first side of a triangle is s cm long.
   The second side is twice as long as the first.
   The third side is 5 cm longer than the second side.
   a The perimeter of the triangle is 1 metre.
      Write an equation to show this.
   b Solve the equation.
   c Find the length of the longest side of the triangle.

4. Read what Sasha says.

   > I am y years old.
   > My mother's age is 3 times my age.
   > My brother is 2 years younger than me.
   > My father's age is 4 times my brother's age.
   > The total of our four ages is 116 years.

   a Write an equation to show this.
   b Solve the equation.
   c How old is Sasha's father?

5. Jake is thinking of a number.

   > If you subtract 8 from my number and multiply by 5, you get the same answer as if you add 10 to my number and multiply by 2.

   a Write an equation to show this.
   b Find the original number.

6. The length of one side of a rectangle is a cm.
   Another side is $3(a-2)$ cm long.
   The perimeter is 44 cm.
   a Write an equation to show this.
   b Find the lengths of the sides of the rectangle.

Exercise 13.3 Simultaneous equations 1

1. Solve these simultaneous equations.
   $y = 3x$
   $y = x + 12$

2. Solve these simultaneous equations.
   $y = 3 - x$
   $y = 2x - 15$

3. Solve these simultaneous equations.
   $y = 2x + 1$
   $y = -2x + 9$

4. Solve these simultaneous equations.
   a $x + y = 30$
       $y = 4x$
   b $2x + y = 14$
       $y = x + 2$
   c $x + y = -2$
       $y = 2x - 5$

5. Look at these simultaneous equations.

   $2x + 3y = 23$
   $5x + 2y = 30$

   Show that the solution is $x = 4$ and $y = 5$.

6. Solve these simultaneous equations.
   $y = 2x$
   $x = y - 10$

7. Solve these simultaneous equations.
   $y = 4(x + 3)$
   $x + y = 20$

8. Solve these simultaneous equations.
   $3y + 2x = 1$
   $y = 5 - x$

9. Solve these simultaneous equations.
   $y = 12 + 4x$
   $x + 2y = 6$

Exercise 13.4 Simultaneous equations 2

1. Solve each pair of simultaneous equations.
   a. $x + y = 20$
      $x - y = 16$
   b. $a + b = 15$
      $a - b = 4$
   c. $q - p = 12$
      $p + q = 4$

2. Solve these simultaneous equations.
   a. $3x + y = 30$
      $2x - y = 15$
   b. $x + 2y = 21$
      $3x - 2y = 15$

3. Solve these simultaneous equations.
   a. $y + 2x = 15$
      $y + 4x = 20$
   b. $3x + 2y = 64$
      $2y + x = 40$

4. Look at these three equations.

   $x + y = 13$
   $x - y = 2$
   $2x + y = 19$

   a. Solve the first two simultaneously.
   b. Show that it is not possible to solve all three equations simultaneously.

5. Solve these equations simultaneously.
   a. $2x - y = 2$
      $y = 3x - 8$
   b. $y = 2(x - 2)$
      $2x + y = 10$
   c. $2a - 3b = 9$
      $2a + 3b = 3$

Exercise 13.5 Trial and improvement

1. Find a positive integer solution for each equation.
   a $x^2 - x = 72$
   b $x^2 + 2x = 120$
   c $4x + x^2 = 21$

2. Look at this equation.

   $x^2 + 10x = 162.69$

   It has a solution between 8 and 10.
   Use trial and improvement to find the solution.

3. Look at this equation.
   $x(x + 3) = 19.84$
   It has a solution between 1 and 5.
   Use trial and improvement to find the solution.

4. Use trial and improvement to find a positive solution to each equation.
   a $x^2 + 2x = 2.61$
   b $x^2 + 2x = 181.25$

5. Maha is practising trial and improvement.

   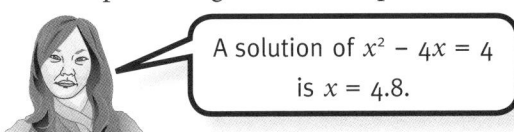

   A solution of $x^2 - 4x = 4$ is $x = 4.8$.

   Show that her answer is correct, to one decimal place.

6. Look at this equation.
   $x^2 + 3x = 12$
   Use trial and improvement to solve the equation.
   Give your answer correct to one decimal place.
   Put your trials in a table.

7. Look at this equation.
   $x^3 + x = 22$
   Use trial and improvement to solve the equation.
   Give your answer correct to one decimal place.

8. Look at this equation.
   $6x - x^2 = 7$
   The equation has <u>two</u> solutions between 1 and 5.
   Use trial and improvement to find both solutions.
   Give your answers correct to one decimal place.

Exercise 13.6 Inequalities

1 Write down the inequality for each solution set.

   a
   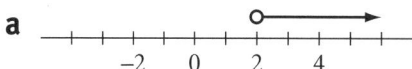

   b

   c

   d

2 Show each inequality on a number line.
   a $x \geq -2$ **b** $x < 3.5$
   c $x \leq -3$ **d** $10 > x$

3 N is an integer and $N \leq 4$.
   For each each statement say whether it:
   Must be true   Could be true   Cannot be true.
   a $N = 4$ **b** $N < 0$
   c $N < 5$ **d** $N \geq 5$

4 Solve these inequalities.
   a $10x \geq 5$ **b** $4x + 10 < 22$
   c $5(x - 7) \leq 30$ **d** $15 > 2(x + 1)$

5 Solve these inequalities.
   a $4x - 5 \leq 2x + 15$
   b $x + 6 > 14 - x$
   c $5(2 + x) \leq 10x$

6 Xavier had 100 dollars.
   He gave A dollars to his brother.
   He gave his sister 5 dollars more than he gave his brother.
   He gave his friend twice as much as he gave his sister.
   He still had some money left.
   a Write down an inequality for A.
   b Solve the inequality.
   c Explain why he could not have given his friend 55 dollars.

7 The angles of a quadrilateral add up to 360 degrees.
   Three of the angles, in degrees are x, $2x$ and $3(x - 10)$.
   a Write down an inequality for x.
   b Solve the inequality.
   c Could the angles that are $2x$ degrees and $3(x - 10)$ degrees be the same size?
      Give a reason for your answer.

14 Ratio and proportion

◆ Exercise 14.1 Comparing and using ratios

1. Gemma mixes two shades of yellow paint.
   She uses the following ratios of yellow : white.

   > Banana yellow 5 : 3   Mellow yellow 7 : 5

   a Write each ratio in the form 1 : n.
   b Which type of yellow paint is the lighter shade?

2. Gavin mixes a drink.
   He uses orange juice and pineapple juice in the ratio 2 : 7.
   Matt mixes a drink.
   He uses orange juice and pineapple juice in the ratio 3 : 10.
   a Write each ratio in the form 1 : n.
   b Who has made the drink with the higher proportion of pineapple juice?

3. Adalyn has a silver bracelet that is made from 1.7 g of copper and 22.3 g of silver.
   a Write the ratio of copper to silver in the form 1 : n.
   Raine has a silver bracelet that is made from 1.8 g of copper and 28.2 g of silver.
   b Write the ratio of copper to silver in the form 1 : n.
   c Whose silver bracelet has the higher proportion of silver?

4. There are 27 boys and 38 girls in the Bounders athletics club.
   a Write the ratio of boys to girls, in the form 1 : n.
   There are 35 boys and 47 girls in the Jumpers athletics club.
   b Write the ratio of boys to girls, in the form 1 : n.
   c Which athletics club has the higher proportion of girls?

5. When Oria makes cookies she uses butter and sugar in the ratio 2 : 3.
   Oria uses 450 g of sugar to make some cookies.
   What mass of butter does she use?

6. Tyler is a builder.
   When he makes mortar, he uses cement, lime and
   sand in the ratio 1 : 2 : 8.
   For one job Tyler used 20 kg of sand.
   a How much cement and lime did he use?
   b What is the total mass of the mortar he made?

7 The table shows the child-to-staff ratios used by an activity centre for various activities.

Activity	Child : staff ratio	Number of children
Horse-riding	4 : 1	22
Sailing	5 : 1	17
Rock-climbing	8 : 1	30
Canoeing	10 : 1	26

It also shows the number of children taking part in each activity on one day.
Each activity takes place at the same time, in a different area of the activity centre.
What is the total number of staff needed to look after the children at the activity centre on this day?

8 This is part of Hassan's homework.

> *Question*   Alice and Joe share $520 in the ratio 2 : 3.
> How much does Alice receive?
> *Answer*   2 + 3 = 5 parts
> 520 ÷ 5 = $104 per part
> Alice receives = 2 × 104 = $208
> *Check*   Joe receives = 3 × 104 = $312,
> so total = 208 + 312 = $520 ✓

Solve the following problems.
Use Hassan's method of checking to make sure your answer is correct.
  a Tipo and Sandra share $1674 in the ratio 4 : 5.
     How much does Tipo receive?
  b Anita, Barry and Chloe share $900 in the ratio 2 : 3 : 7.
     How much does Chloe receive?
  c Mika, Nova and Catori share $2340 in the ratio 5 : 2 : 8.
     How much does Nova receive?
  d Eric, Astrid, Lucas and Ricardo share €1410 in the ratio of their ages.
     Eric is 11 years old, Astrid is 15 years old, Lucas is 16 years old and Ricardo is 18 years old.
     How much does Eric receive?

9 Every year a grandmother gives $350 to her granddaughters to be shared in the ratio of their ages.
This year her two granddaughters are 8 years old and 11 years old.
  a How much will the younger granddaughter receive in three years' time?
  b Show how to check your answer to part **a**.

◆ Exercise 14.2 Solving problems

1. Are these quantities in direct proportion?
   Give reasons for your answers.
   a The total cost of bottles of lemonade and the number of bottles bought
   b The number of girls in a swimming club and the number of boys in a swimming club
   c The total cost of stamps and the number of stamps bought
   d The distance travelled in an aeroplane and the time taken to travel that distance
   e The number of students in a mathematics class and the students' shoe sizes
   f The amount of homework a student does in an evening and the number of brothers and sisters they have

2. Sam is paid $100 for working 8 hours.
   How much is he paid for working:
   a 4 hours
   b 6 hours
   c 15 hours?

3. Six bags of sweets cost $11.10.
   a How much do 18 bags of sweets cost?
   b How much do 11 bags of sweets cost?

4. A shop sells tea bags in boxes of 80 and in boxes of 120.
   A box of 80 tea bags costs $2.36.
   a Work out the cost of 40 of these tea bags.
   A box of 120 tea bags $3.45.
   b Work out the cost of 40 of these tea bags.
   c Which box of tea bags is better value for money?

5. This is part of Harsha's homework.

   > *Question* A 500 g jar of pasta sauce costs $1.84.
   > A 350 g jar of pasta sauce costs $1.26.
   > Which jar is better value for money?
   > *Answer* 1.84 ÷ 5 = $0.368 for 100 g.
   > *Check* 5 × 0.368 = $1.84
   > 1.26 ÷ 3.5 = $0.36 for 100 g.
   > *Check* 3.5 × 0.36 = $1.26
   > The 350 g jar is better value for money.

   I have used inverse operations to check each calculation.

   Use Harsha's method of checking when you solve these problems.
   Show all your working.
   a A box of 50 pens costs $11.75.
      A box of 80 pens costs $19.20.
      Which box gives you better value for money?
   b A 500 g pack of cereal costs $2.85.
      A 750 g pack of cereal costs $4.25.
      Which pack gives you better value for money?
   c A 350 ml pot of yoghurt costs $0.69.
      A 450 ml pot of yoghurt costs $0.86.
      Which pot gives better value for money?

6 Zac travelled from the US to the UK when the exchange rate was $1 = £0.65.
He changed $320 into British pounds (£).
How many pounds did he get?

7 Frieda travelled between Australia and Singapore when the exchange rate was A$1 = S$1.15.
  a When she went to Singapore she changed A$450 into Singapore dollars (S$).
  How many Singapore dollars did she get?
  b When she returned to Australia she changed S$120 into Australian dollars (A$).
  How many Australian dollars did she get?
  Give your answer to the nearest dollar.

8 Paul travelled from the US to France when the exchange rate was €0.78 = $1.
He saw a mobile phone in a shop in Paris for €187.
The same mobile phone cost $254 in New York.
Where should Paul buy the mobile phone?
Show your working and check your answer.

15 Area, perimeter and volume

◆ Exercise 15.1 Converting units of area and volume

1. Convert these measures.
   - **a** 7 m² to cm²
   - **b** 0.8 m² to cm²
   - **c** 3.25 m² to cm²
   - **d** 5 cm² to mm²
   - **e** 0.4 cm² to mm²
   - **f** 9.2 cm² to mm²
   - **g** 90 000 cm² to m²
   - **h** 34 000 cm² to m²
   - **i** 5000 cm² to m²
   - **j** 300 mm² to cm²
   - **k** 280 mm² to cm²
   - **l** 80 mm² to cm²

2. Convert these measures.
   - **a** 2 m³ to cm³
   - **b** 0.24 m³ to cm³
   - **c** 5.6 m³ to cm³
   - **d** 8 cm³ to mm³
   - **e** 0.5 cm³ to mm³
   - **f** 7.2 cm³ to mm³
   - **g** 9 000 000 cm³ to m³
   - **h** 480 000 cm³ to m³
   - **i** 82 200 000 cm³ to m³
   - **j** 7000 mm³ to cm³
   - **k** 230 mm³ to cm³
   - **l** 77 600 mm³ to cm³

3. Convert these measures.
   - **a** 70 cm³ to ml
   - **b** 348 cm³ to ml
   - **c** 2500 cm³ to ml
   - **d** 7000 cm³ to litres
   - **e** 8400 cm³ to litres
   - **f** 920 cm³ to litres
   - **g** 8 litres to cm³
   - **h** 3.9 litres to cm³
   - **i** 0.88 litres to cm³

4. Amanda's bedroom is a rectangle 415 cm long by 295 cm wide.
   - **a** Work out the area of Amanda's bedroom. Give your answer in square metres (m²). Show how to use estimation to check your answer.

   Carpet costs $24 per square metre.
   It is sold in whole numbers of square metres.
   - **b** How much will it cost Amanda to buy carpet for her bedroom floor? Show how to use inverse operations to check your answer.

5. Greg is going to paint the four walls of his lounge.
   The diagram shows the dimensions of the walls.
   The shaded regions are the parts of the walls that need painting.

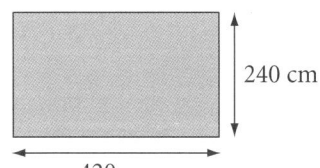
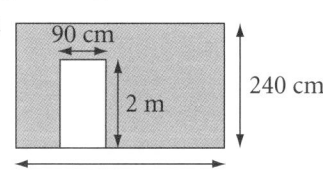
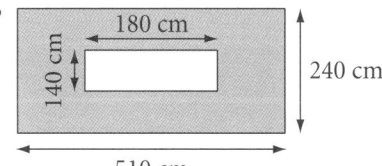
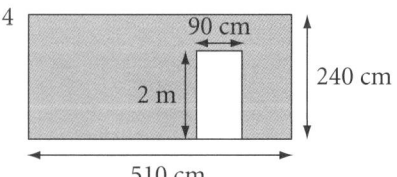

What is the total area of wall, in square metres, that Greg will paint?
Show how to check your answer.

Exercise 15.2 Using hectares

1 Copy and complete these statements.
   a 4 ha = ☐ m²
   b 5.2 ha = ☐ m²
   c 0.9 ha = ☐ m²
   d 45.2 ha = ☐ m²
   e 0.82 ha = ☐ m²
   f 0.034 ha = ☐ m²

2 Copy and complete these statements.
   a 70 000 m² = ☐ ha
   b 32 000 m² = ☐ ha
   c 670 000 m² = ☐ ha
   d 8800 m² = ☐ ha
   e 700 m² = ☐ ha
   f 2 375 000 m² = ☐ ha

3 A rectangular piece of land measures 420 m by 360 m.
   Work out the area of the land.
   Give your answer in:
   a square metres (m²)
   b hectares (ha).

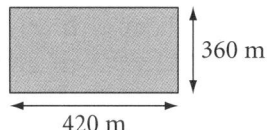

4 Work out the area of this triangular piece of land.
   Give your answer in:
   a square metres (m²)
   b hectares (ha).

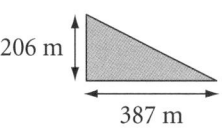

5 A farmer has a T-shaped field.
   The dimensions of the field are shown in the diagram.
   a Work out the area of the field, in square metres (m²).
   b Work out the area of the field, in hectares (ha).
   The farmer sells the field for $2200 per hectare.
   c How much money does the farmer receive?
   d Show how to use estimation to check your answer.

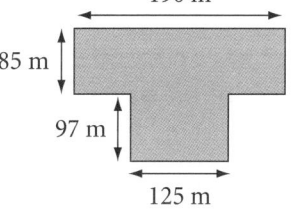

6 A builder wants to buy a plot of land to build houses.
   The shape of the land is shown in the diagram.
   He wants to spend no more than $40 000 for the land.
   The plot of land is on sale for $3900 per hectare.
   Can the builder afford to buy the land?
   Show all your working.
   Use estimation to check your answer.

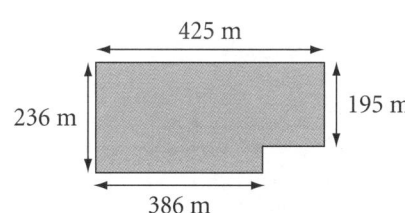

15 Area, perimeter and volume

Exercise 15.3   Solving circle problems

1. Work out the area (*A*) and the circumference (*C*) of each circle.
   Give your answers correct to one decimal place (1 d.p.).
   a radius = 2 cm
   b radius = 4.6 m
   c diameter = 18 cm
   d diameter = 5.2 m

   Throughout this exercise use the 'π' button on your calculator.

2. Work out the area (*A*) and the perimeter (*P*) of each semicircle.
   Give your answers correct to one decimal place (1 d.p.).
   a radius = 8.5 cm
   b radius = 24 mm
   c diameter = 32 cm
   d diameter = 15 m

3. Work out the diameter (*d*) of each circle.
   Give your answers correct to two decimal places (2 d.p.).
   a circumference = 26.3 cm
   b circumference = 89.5 mm
   c circumference = 4.75 m
   d circumference = 35.5 cm

4. Work out the radius (*r*) of each circle.
   Give your answers correct to two decimal places (2 d.p.).
   a area = 157 cm^2
   b area = 45.8 m^2
   c area = 0.88 m^2
   d area = 365 mm^2

5. A circular coin has a circumference of 8.7 cm.
   Work out the radius of the coin.
   Give your answer correct to the nearest millimetre.

6. A circular patio floor has an area of 45.3 m^2.
   Work out the diameter of the patio floor.
   Give your answer correct to the nearest centimetre.

7. A circular badge has a circumference of 18.5 cm.
   Work out the area of the badge.
   Give your answer correct to the nearest square centimetre.

8. Work out the area of each compound shape.
   Give your answers correct to two decimal places (2 d.p.).

   a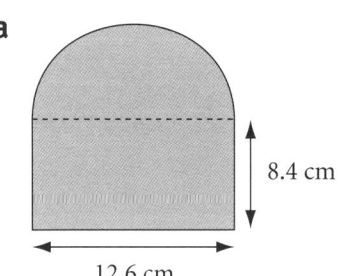
   b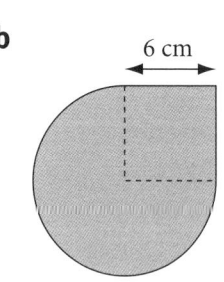

Exercise 15.4 Calculating with prisms and cylinders

1. Work out the volume of each prism. The area of cross-section is given.

   a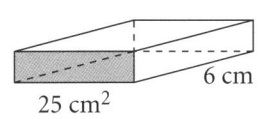

   b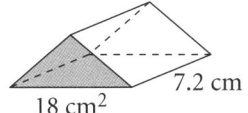

   c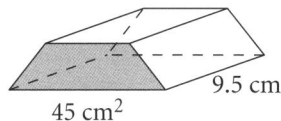

2. Copy and complete this table.

	Area of cross-section	Length of prism	Volume of prism
a	8.4 cm²	20 cm	☐ cm³
b	24 cm²	☐ cm	156 cm³
c	☐ m²	5.7 m	330.6 m³
d	56.85 mm²	☐ mm	3524.7 mm³

3. Work out the volume and surface area of each prism.

   a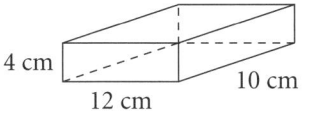

   b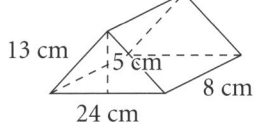

   c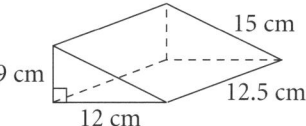

4. Work out the volume and surface area of each cylinder.
   Give your answers correct to one decimal place (1 d.p.).

   a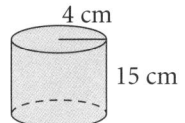

   b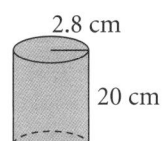

   c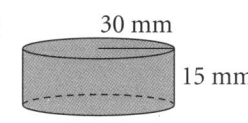

5. Copy and complete this table. Give your answers correct to two decimal places (2 d.p.).

	Radius of circle	Area of circle	Height of cylinder	Volume of cylinder
a	7 cm	☐ cm²	12 cm	☐ cm³
b	1.5 m	☐ m²	2.4 m	☐ m³
c	9 cm	☐ cm²	☐ cm	1910 cm³
d	☐ m	15 m²	3.8 m	☐ m³
e	☐ mm	☐ mm²	22 mm	1430 mm³

6. Each of these prisms has a volume of 335 cm³.
   Work out the value of x in each diagram.
   Give your answers correct to one decimal place (1 d.p.).

   a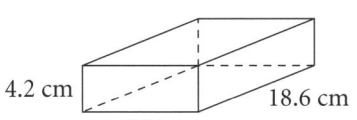

   b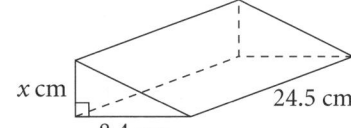

   c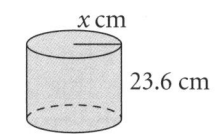

16 Probability

◆ Exercise 16.1 Calculating probabilities

1 Oditi plants six flower seeds.
  The table shows the probabilities for the number of plants that will grow from the six seeds.

Number of plants that will grow	6	5	4
Probability	0.1	0.2	0.25

  Work out the probability that:
  a fewer than 6 plants   b fewer than 5 plants   c fewer than 4 plants will grow.

2 The probability that Alicia's teacher will be on time for a lesson is 0.85.
  The probability that he will be late is 0.1.
  The probability that he will be absent is 0.05.
  Find the probability that Alicia's teacher will:
  a <u>not</u> be absent   b <u>not</u> be late   c <u>not</u> be present at the start of the lesson.

3 An aeroplane is due to depart at 13:00.
  It will definitely not depart before 13:00.
  It may be cancelled.
  The table shows the probabilities for its departure times.

Time of departure	13:00–13:30	13:30–14:00	14:00–15:00	After 15:00
Probability	25%	55%	10%	5%

  Find the probability that the departure will be:
  a cancelled   b less than one hour late   c after 14:00.

4 This table shows the probability that one or more buses will arrive at the library in the next hour.

Number of buses	1	2	More than 2
Probability	0.65	0.15	0.05

  Work out the probability of:
  a no buses   b at least 1 bus   c at least 2 buses arriving at the library.

5 Two spinners each have a number 4 on them.
  The probability that neither shows 4 is $\frac{9}{16}$. The probability just one shows 4 is $\frac{3}{8}$.
  Find the probability of
  a two 4s   b at least one 4.

6 Xavier throws a normal dice until it shows a 6.
  The probability this takes more than one throw is 0.83.
  The probability this takes more than two throws is 0.69.
  The probability this takes more that three throws is 0.58.
  Find the probability it takes:
  a one throw   b one or two throws   c exactly three throws.

Exercise 16.2 Sample space diagrams

1. Sasha spins two coins together.
   a Draw a sample space diagram to show all the possible results.
   b Use it to explain why Sasha is twice as likely to throw one head and one tail as two heads.

2. Anders throws two dice together.
   a Draw a sample space diagram to show all the possible results.
   b Work out the probability of Anders' throwing:
      i at least one 5
      ii the same number on both dice
      iii numbers with a difference of 2.

3. Mia has two spinners.
   One has four numbers: 0, 2, 4, 6.
   The other has three numbers: 2, 3, 4.
   Mia spins the two spinners together.
   a Draw a sample space diagram to show all the possible results.
   b Find the probability that:
      i both numbers are the same
      ii the total is more than 3
      iii the difference is more than 3.

4. Dakarai makes up two sets of three cards.
   Each set has one card with letter A on it, one with letter B and one with letter C.
   Dakarai gives two people a full set of cards each and asks them to take one card.
   a Draw a sample space diagram to show all the possible results.
   b Find the probability that:
      i both pick the same letter
      ii each picks a different letter.

5. Dakarai adds a card to each set he made for question 4.
   Now there are four cards in each set, with the letters A, B, C and D.
   Again, Dakarai gives two people a full set of cards each and asks them to take one card.
   a Draw a sample space diagram to show all the possible results with four cards.
   b Find the probability that:
      i both pick the same letter
      ii each picks a different letter.

6. Look at the answers to questions 4b and 5b.
   Find the same probabilities for five cards.

7. Tanesha chooses a letter from the word GATE.
   Zalika chooses a letter from the word GOAT.
   Find the probability that they choose:
   a the same letter
   b different letters.

   > Draw a sample space diagram.

8. A computer generates two random one-digit numbers from 0, 1, 2, 3, 4, 5, 6, 7, 8 and 9.
   Find the probability that:
   a the numbers are the same
   b the difference between the numbers is 1
   c the difference between the numbers is 2.

◆ Exercise 16.3 Using relative frequency

1 In a survey, a car dealer recorded the cars that passed his office during one morning.
He noted the regions where the cars were made.
The table shows his results.

Region	Europe	Asia	America	Other
Frequency	37	52	16	7

Estimate the probability that a car that passed his office was:
a made in Asia
b <u>not</u> made in Europe
c <u>not</u> made in Asia or Europe.

2 A health worker weighed the students in two schools.
The table shows the numbers of students who were normal, overweight or underweight.

	Normal	Overweight	Underweight
School A	125	32	17
School B	294	61	29

a Estimate the probability that a student from each school is:
  i normal
  ii overweight
  iii underweight.
b Which school has healthier students?
  Give a reason for your answer.

3 This table shows the weather in a city on 1 July each year for the past 50 years.

Weather	Hot and sunny	Cloudy and dry	Light rain	Heavy rain
Frequency	32	8	7	3

Estimate the probability that this year 1 July will be:
a hot and sunny
b dry.

4 A hotel booking website asked customers to give a grade to any hotel they used.
The grades went from from 1 (poor) to 5 (excellent).
Here are the results for two hotels.

	Grade				
	1	2	3	4	5
City Hotel	3	6	24	27	16
Mountain View Hotel	4	19	67	26	18

a Find the probability that each hotel will get a grade 1 or 2.
b Find the probability that each hotel will get a grade 4 or 5.
c Which hotel got better grades?
  Give a reason for your answer.

5 Trains travel to Central City in the morning and in the afternoon.
This table shows when they arrived one week.

	Number of trains that were...			
	...early	...on time	...less than 5 minutes late	...more than 5 minutes late
Morning	4	31	6	7
Afternoon	2	52	7	3

a Find the probability that:
  i a morning train is late   **ii** an afternoon train is late.
b Which trains have a better record for being on time?

6 City and United are two football teams.
They have played each other 24 times in the past ten years.
Here are the results.

Result	Win for City	Win for United	Draw
Frequency	14	4	6

a Use the table to estimate the probability that in the next match:
  i City will win   **ii** City will lose.
b Read what Jake says.

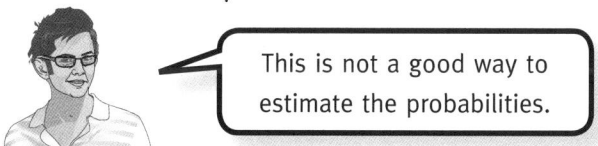

> This is not a good way to estimate the probabilities.

Do you agree?
Give a reason for your answer.

17 Bearings and scale drawings

◆ **Exercise 17.1 Using bearings**

1. The diagram shows the position of a park and a library.
   a. Measure and write down the bearing of the park from the library.
   b. Write down the bearing of the library from the park.

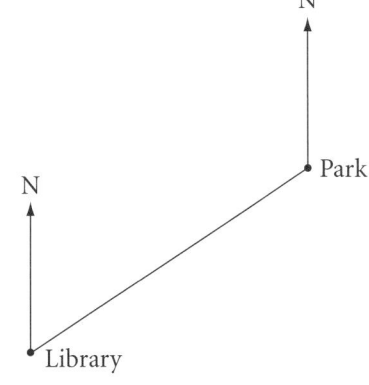

2. Bethan enters an orienteering competition.
   The diagram shows the position of the start and finish and the four checkpoints that Bethan must find.
   Measure and write down the bearing that Bethan takes to run from:
   a. the start to checkpoint 1
   b. checkpoint 1 to checkpoint 2
   c. checkpoint 2 to checkpoint 3
   d. checkpoint 3 to checkpoint 4
   e. checkpoint 4 to the finish.

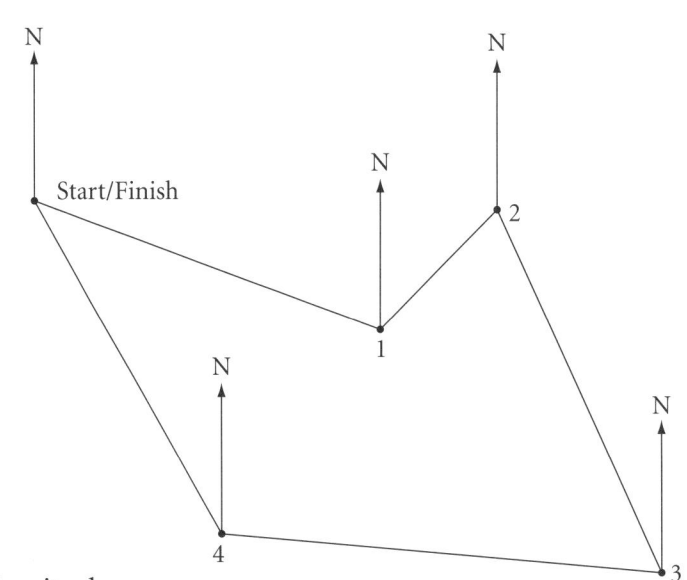

3. a. For each of these diagrams measure and write down:
   i. the bearing of Y from X
   ii. the bearing of X from Y.

   A   **B**   **C**

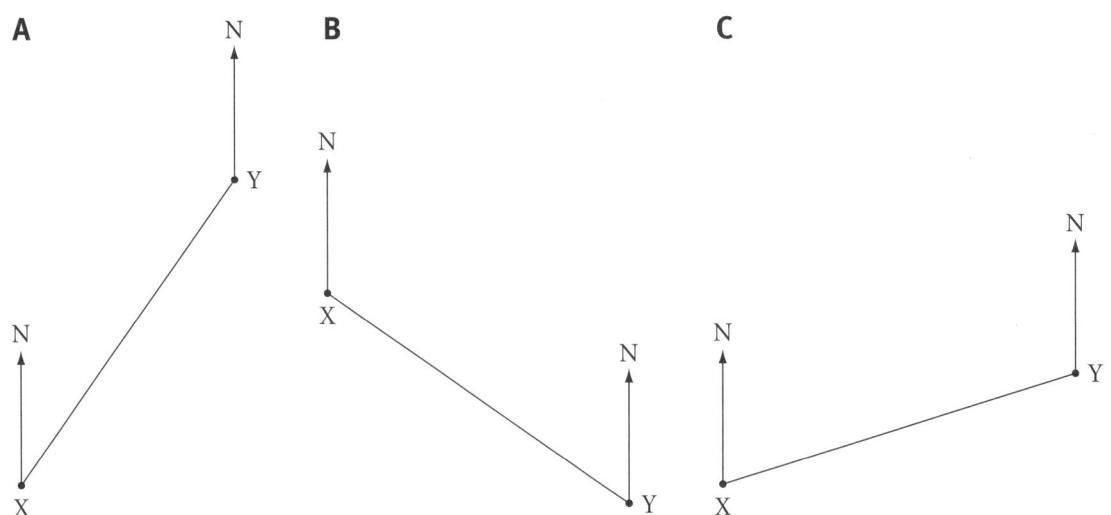

b What do you notice about each pair of answers you found in part **a**?
c For each of these diagrams:
  i write down the bearing of Y from X
  ii work out the bearing of X from Y.

A 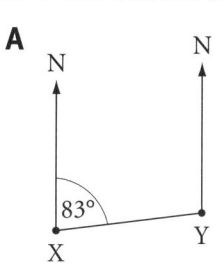   B 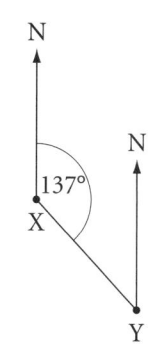   C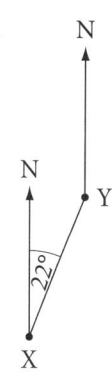

4 a For this diagram, measure and write down:
  i the bearing of X from Y   **ii** the bearing of Y from X.

A 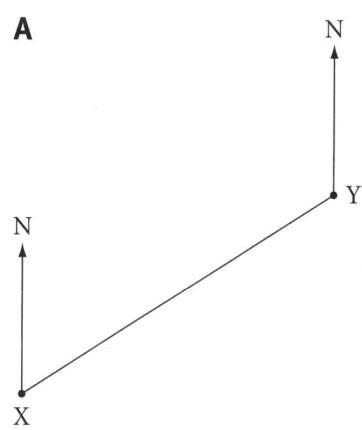   B 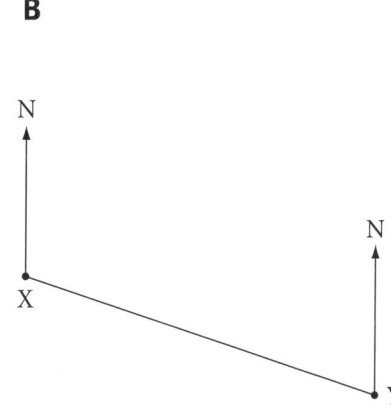   C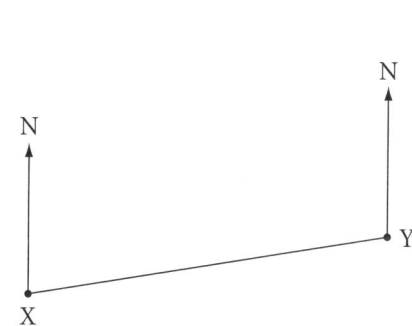

b What do you notice about each pair of answers you have found in part **a**?
c For each of these diagrams:
  i write down the bearing of X from Y   **ii** work out the bearing of Y from X.

A 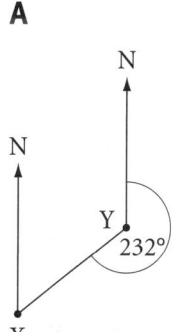   B 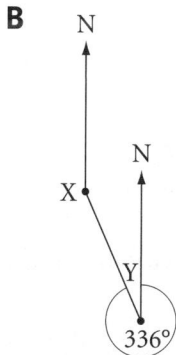   C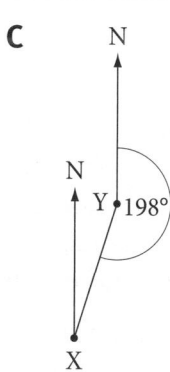

◆ Exercise 17.2 Making scale drawings

1. A ship leaves harbour and sails 125 km on a bearing of 080°.
   It then sails 85 km on a bearing of 145°.
   a Make a scale drawing of the ship's journey.
   b How far must the ship now sail to return to the harbour?
   c On what bearing must the ship now sail to return to the harbour?

   Use a scale of 1 cm to represent 10 km.

2. An aeroplane leaves an airport and flies 240 km on a bearing of 300°.
   It then changes direction and flies 120 km on a bearing of 190°.
   a Make a scale drawing of the aeroplane's journey.
   b How far must the aeroplane now fly to return to the airport?
   c On what bearing must the aeroplane now fly to return to the airport?

   Use a scale of 1 cm to represent 20 km.

3. Greg leaves his car and walks 16 km on a bearing of 095°.
   He then changes direction and walks 14 km on a bearing of 035°.
   a Make a scale drawing of Greg's walk.
   b How far must Greg now walk to return to his car?
   c On what bearing must Greg now walk to return to his car?

   Use a scale of 1 cm to represent 2 km.

4. Li lives 10 km west of Chul.
   Li leaves home and walks 8 km to a farm.
   He walks on a bearing of 137°.
   Chul leaves home and walks to meet Li at the farm.
   How far, and on what bearing, does he walk?

   Make scale drawings to work out the answers to questions 4 and 5.
   You will need to decide what scales to use.

5. At noon, a yacht is 55 km south of a ship.
   The yacht sails on a bearing of 335°.
   The ship sails on a bearing of 212°.
   Could the yacht and the ship collide?
   Explain your answer.

6. The scale on a map is 1 : 50 000.
   a On the map, a river is 48 cm long.
      What is the length, in kilometres, of the actual river?
   b The actual length of a lake is 7 km.
      What is the length, in centimetres, of the lake on the map?

   The actual distance is the distance in real life.

7. The scale on a map is 1 : 800 000.
   a On the map, the distance between two cities is 32 cm.
      What is the actual distance, in kilometres, between the two cities?
   b The actual distance between two towns is 46 km.
      What is the distance, in centimetres, between the two towns on the map?

8. Zahra participated in a charity fun run.
   The table shows the distances, on the map, between consecutive checkpoints on the run.
   The scale of the map is 1 : 25 000.
   Zahra raised $36 for charity for every kilometre she ran.
   What was the total amount that Zahra raised for charity?

Checkpoints	Distance on map (cm)
Start to 1	12
1 to 2	9.5
2 to 3	14.6
3 to Finish	13.9

18 Graphs

Exercise 18.1 Gradient of a graph

1 Work out the gradient of each line on this coordinate grid.

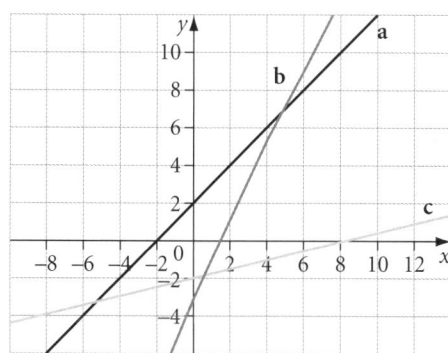

2 Work out the gradient of each line on this coordinate grid.

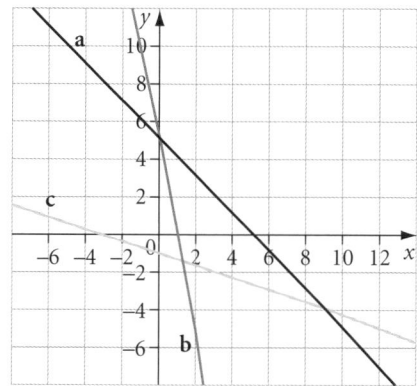

3 a Draw a coordinate grid and mark the point (3, 0).
  b Draw a line through (3, 0), with a gradient of 0.5.
  c Draw a line through (3, 0), with a gradient of −0.5.

4 a Draw a coordinate grid.
  b Draw a line through the origin, with a gradient of 2.
  c Draw a line through (0, 4), with a gradient of 2.
  d Draw a line through (5, 3), with a gradient of 2.

5 Find the gradient of the straight line through each set of points.
  a (0, 0), (2, 5), (−3, −7.5)
  b (0, 6), (4, 0), (8, −6)
  c (−8, −7), (−6, −6), (−2, −4)
  d (−4, 12), (1, −13), (−2, 2)

6 Work out the gradient of each line on this coordinate grid.

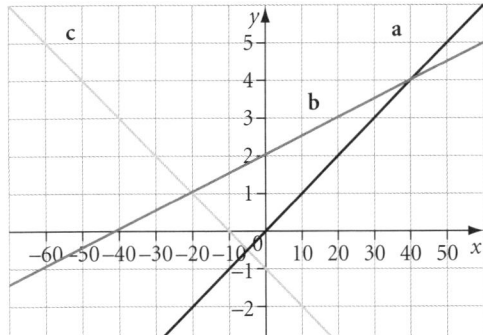

7 Find the gradient of the straight line through each set of points.
   a (0, 0), (2, 50), (4, 100)
   b (0, −5), (20, −3), (30, −2), (60, 1)
   c (10, 45), (25, 30), (40, 15), (60, −5)
   d (30, −30), (45, 0), (60, 30)

Exercise 18.2 The graph of $y = mx + c$

1. **a** On one coordinate grid, draw the lines with these equations.
   i $y = 4x$ **ii** $y = 4x + 2$ **iii** $y = 4x - 6$
   b Find the gradient of each line.

2. These are the equations of four lines.
   A $y = 3x - 2$ **B** $y = 2x - 3$ **C** $y = -4x + 3$ **D** $y = -3x + 4$
   Write down:
   a the letters of lines with positive gradient
   b the gradient of the steepest line
   c the letters of the lines that pass through (1, 1).

3. This is the equation of a straight line.

   $y = 7 - 2x$

   a Find the equation of a line parallel to it and passing through the origin.
   b Find the equation of a line parallel to it and passing through (0, −4).
   c Find the equation of a line parallel to it and passing through (0, 4).

4. A line has the equation $y = 50 - 10x$.
   a Show that the line passes through (0, 50) and (5, 0).
   b Find the gradient of the line.
   c Find the equation of a line parallel to it and passing through (0, 0).

5. Find the gradients of the lines with these equations.
   a $y = 50 - 25x$ **b** $y = 25x - 50$ **c** $y = 25 + 50x$ **d** $y = 75x$

6. These are the equations of five lines.
   Which lines are parallel?
   A $y = 0.1x + 0.2$ **B** $y = 0.2x + 0.1$ **C** $y = 0.1x + 0.1w$
   D $y = 0.1x - 0.2$ **E** $y = 0.2x - 0.1$

Exercise 18.3 Drawing graphs

1. **a** Rearrange these equations into the form $y = mx + c$.
   - **i** $x + y = 12$
   - **ii** $2x + y = 12$
   - **iii** $x + 2y = 12$

   b Each of the equations in part **a** is the equation of a straight line. Find the gradient of each line.

2. This is the equation of a straight line.

   $1.5x - y = 3$

   a Write the equation in the form $y = mx + c$.
   b Draw a graph of the line.
   c Find the gradient of the line.

3. Here is a formula.

   $x = 10y - 14$

   a Rearrange the formula to show it is the equation of a straight line.
   b Find the gradient of the line.

4. These are the equations of straight lines.
   Find the gradient of each one.
   a $2y = 3x + 4$ **b** $5y = 6 - 2x$ **c** $3x + 3y + 4 = 0$ **d** $y - 5x = 1$

5. The equation of one line on this coordinate grid is $5x + 8y = 40$.

   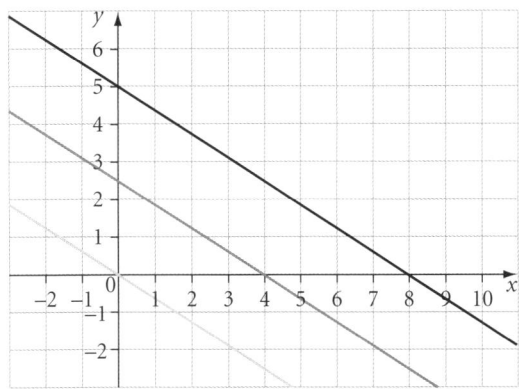

   All three lines are parallel.
   a Match the equation to the correct line on the diagram.
   b Find the equations of the other two lines.

6. The equation of a straight line is $x + 100 = 20y$.
   a Write the equation in the form $y = mx + c$.
   b Find the gradient of the line.
   c Draw a graph of the line.

7. Find the gradients of lines with these equations.
   a $10x + y = 50$ **b** $x + 10y = 50$
   c $50x - y = 10$ **d** $x - 50y = 10$

8. The equation of a straight line is $2.4x + 3.6y = 7.2$.
   a Find the gradient of the line.
   b The line passes through the points $(0, c)$ and $(d, 0)$.
   Find the values of c and d.

Exercise 18.4 Simultaneous equations

1 Use the graph to solve these equations simultaneously.

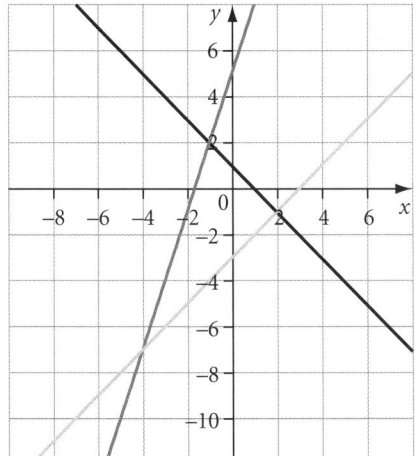

  a $y = x - 3$ and $y = 3x + 5$
  b $y = 3x + 5$ and $y = 1 - x$
  c $y = 1 - x$ and $y = x - 3$

2 Use the graph to find approximate solutions to these equations.

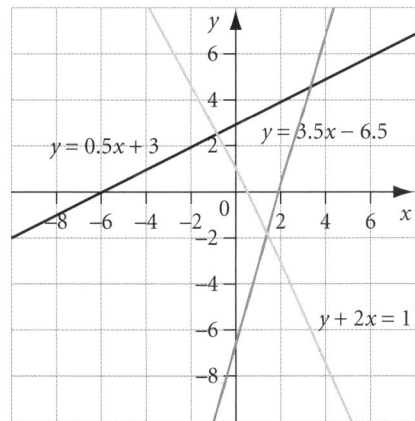

  a $y = 0.5x + 3$ and $y = 3.5x - 6.5$
  b $y + 2x = 1$ and $y = 0.5x + 3$
  c $y = 3.5x - 6.5$ and $y + 2x = 1$

3 a Write these equations in the form $y = mx + c$.
　　i $x + y = 5$　　**ii** $x = y + 3$
b Draw graphs of the lines with these equations.
　Put them on the same grid.
　　i $x + y = 5$　　**ii** $x = y + 3$
c Use the graph to solve the equations $x + y = 5$ and $x = y + 3$ simultaneously.
d Check your answer by solving the equations algebraically.

4 a Draw a graph of the line with equation $x + 2y = 9$.
b On the same axes draw the line with equation $4x + y + 6 = 0$.
c Use your graph to solve the equations $x + 2y = 9$ and $4x + y + 6 = 0$ simultaneously.

5 a Copy these axes.

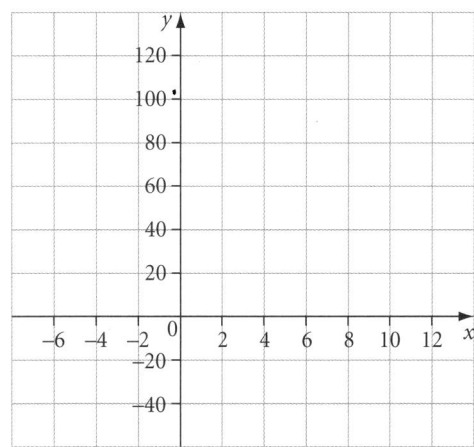

b On the axes, draw graphs of these equations.
　　i $y = 10x + 40$　　**ii** $20x + y = 100$　　**iii** $5x + y = 40$
c Use your graph to solve these equations simultaneously.
　　i $y = 10x + 40$ and $20x + y = 100$
　　ii $20x + y = 100$ and $5x + y = 40$

6 Use a graphical method to find approximate solutions to these simultaneous equations.
$y = 1.5x - 6$ and $4x + 5y = 9$

◆ Exercise 18.5 Direct proportion

1. The exchange rate for euros (€) and dollars ($) is €1 = $1.64.
   a. Draw a graph to illustrate this.
      Put euros on the horizontal axis and dollars on the vertical axis.
      Show amounts up to €100.
   b. What is the gradient of the graph?
   c. Write a formula for the number of dollars (D) in terms of the number of euros (E).
   d. Use the formula to convert:
      i €295 into dollars
      ii $295 into euros.

2. Saffron is a very expensive spice.
   A shop is selling saffron for $7.35 per gram.
   a. Draw a graph showing the cost of up to 5 grams.
   b. Write a formula for the cost (y), in dollars, of g grams of saffron.
   c. Use the formula to find:
      i the cost of 3.4 grams
      ii the number of grams you can buy for $20.

3. A large aeroplane uses about 250 litres of fuel per minute.
   a. How much fuel does it use in 1 hour?
   b. Draw a graph to show the fuel used for up to 1 hour.
      Put minutes on the horizontal scale.
   c. Write down a formula for the number (f) of litres of fuel used in m minutes.
   d. Use the formula to find:
      i the amount of fuel used in a flight lasting 2 hours and 45 minutes
      ii the time it takes to use 100 000 litres of fuel.

4. Hair grows at a rate of about 0.3 cm per week.
   a. Draw a graph to show the length of a new hair, in centimetres, for the first 12 weeks.
   b. What is the gradient of the graph?
   c. Write down a formula for the length (l), in centimetres, of a new hair after w weeks.
   d. How long will it take for a hair to grow to one metre long?

5. At the 1995 World Snail Racing Championships, a snail named Archie covered a 33 cm course in 2 minutes.
   a. Draw a graph to show how far Archie travels in the 2 minutes.
      Assume he travels at a constant speed.
   b. Find the gradient of the graph.
   c. How long does Archie take to travel one metre?

◆ Exercise 18.6 Practical graphs

1. Bamboo is one of the fastest growing plants in the world.
   When a gardener measured a bamboo cane it was 2.0 metres high.
   This type of bamboo grows 0.5 metres each day.
   a Write a formula for the height (h), in metres, d days after it was first measured.
   b Draw a graph of the height.
   c Use the graph to find:
      i   the height after 4 days   ii the time until the height is 6.5 metres.

2. Zalika is saving up her money.

   I have 20 dollars.
   I save 3 dollars every week.

   a Write a formula for the total amount (D), in dollars, Zalika has saved after w weeks.
   b Draw a graph to show the total amount saved.
   Number the 'Weeks' axis up to at least 10 and the 'Dollars' axis to 60.
   c Use the graph to find:
      i   the amount after 4 weeks
      ii the time to save 50 dollars.

3. There were 14 000 people at a football match.
   After the game they left the stadium at a rate of 500 every minute.
   a Write a formula for the number (n) of people left in the stadium after m minutes.
   b Draw a graph to show the relationship between n and m.
   c How long will it take until there are only 10 000 people left in the stadium?

4. Alicia is visiting her grandmother.

   My grandmother takes four tablets each day.
   She has 30 tablets left.

   a Write a formula for the number (t) of tablets left after d days.
   b Draw a graph to show t as a function of d.
   c When will Alicia's grandmother run out of tablets?

5. There are 20 000 litres of water in a tank.
   1500 litres are used every day.
   a Write a formula for the number of litres (L) left after d days.
   b Draw a graph to show L as a function of d.
   c How much water is left after 5 days?
   d How long will the water last?

6. At the last census, the population of a country was 25 million.
   Since the census, the population is increasing by 0.1 million every year.
   a Write a formula for the population, P millions, after y years.
   b Draw a graph to show how the population will change over the next 50 years.
   c When will the population be 28 million?

> Let P be measured in millions, to avoid very big numbers.

19 Interpreting and discussing results

◆ Exercise 19.1 Interpreting and drawing frequency diagrams

1 The table shows the times taken by the students in class 9C to complete a cross-country run.
   a How many students are there in class 9C?
   b Copy and complete the table.
   c Draw a frequency polygon for this data.
   d What fraction of the students took less than 14 minutes to complete the run?

Time, t (minutes)	Frequency	Midpoint
$10 \leq t < 12$	4	
$12 \leq t < 14$	16	
$14 \leq t < 16$	7	
$16 \leq t < 18$	5	

2 Mia completed a survey on the heights of people going on a roller-coaster ride at a theme park on two days. The tables show the results of her survey.

Wednesday		
Height, h (cm)	Frequency	Midpoint
$120 \leq h < 140$	4	
$140 \leq h < 160$	6	
$160 \leq h < 180$	22	
$180 \leq h < 200$	18	

Saturday		
Height, h (cm)	Frequency	Midpoint
$120 \leq h < 140$	25	
$140 \leq h < 160$	16	
$160 \leq h < 180$	7	
$180 \leq h < 200$	2	

   a How many people were surveyed on each day?
   b Copy and complete the tables.
   c On the same grid, draw a frequency polygon for each set of data.
      Make sure you show clearly which frequency polygon represents which day.
   d Compare the two frequency polygons. What can you say about the heights of the people on the roller-coaster ride on the two days?

3 Harsha completed a survey on the number of hours that the athletes from two different clubs spend training each week. The frequency diagrams show the results of her survey.

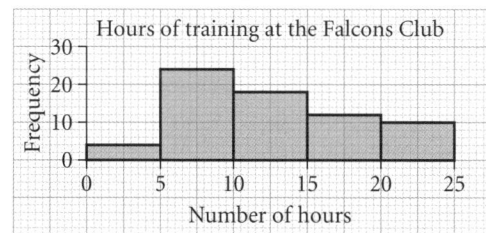
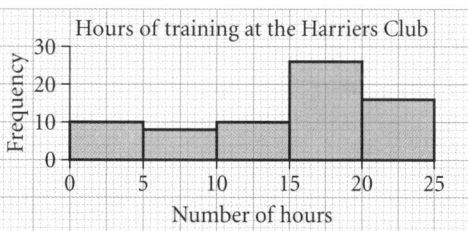

   a On the same grid, draw a frequency polygon for each set of data.
   b Compare the two frequency polygons.
      What can you say about the amounts of time that the athletes from the two different clubs spend training each week?
   c How many athletes from each club were surveyed?
   d Do you think it is fair to make a comparison using these sets of data? Explain your answer.

Exercise 19.2 Interpreting and drawing line graphs

1 The table shows the average monthly rainfall in Faro, Portugal.

Month	Jan	Feb	Mar	Apr	May	Jun	Jul	Aug	Sep	Oct	Nov	Dec
Rainfall (mm)	78	72	39	38	21	8	1	4	14	67	86	94

   a Draw a line graph for this data.
   b Describe the trend in the data.
   c Between which two months was the greatest decrease in rainfall?

2 The table shows a company's profits from 2002 to 2010.
  Each figure is rounded to the nearest $0.1 million.

Year	2002	2004	2006	2008	2010
Profit ($ millions)	5.6	5.9	6.1	6.4	6.6

   a Draw a line graph for this data. Make sure your horizontal axis extends to 2012.
   b Describe the trend in the data.
   c Use your graph to estimate the company's profits in 2005.
   d Use your graph to predict the company's profits in 2012.

3 The table shows the maximum and minimum daily temperatures recorded in Marrakech, Morocco, during one week in July.

Day	Mon	Tues	Wed	Thur	Fri	Sat	Sun
Maximum temperature (°C)	31	32	36	37	34	32	33
Minimum temperature (°C)	18	18	19	22	21	20	17

   a Draw line graphs on the same axes to show this data.
   b Describe the trend in both sets of data.
   c On which day was the difference between the maximum and minimum temperatures greatest?

4 The line graph shows the numbers of visitors to New York City from 2002 to 2010.

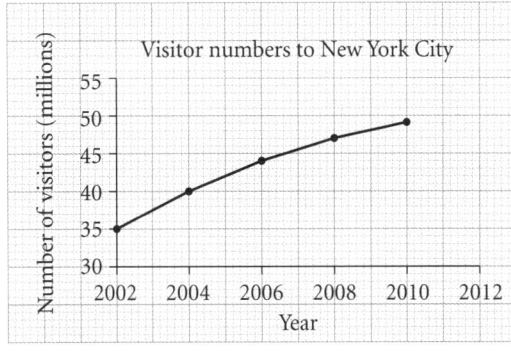

   a Use the graph to estimate the number of visitors to New York City in 2005.
   b Between which two years was the biggest increase in the number of visitors to New York City?
   c Between which two years was the smallest increase in the number of visitors to New York City?
   d Is it possible to use this graph to predict the number of visitors to New York City in 2012? Explain your answer.

◆ Exercise 19.3 Interpreting and drawing scatter graphs

1. Maha carries out a survey on 15 students in her class. She asks them how many hours a week they spend reading, and what they scored in a recent spelling test (out of 20).
   The table shows the results of her survey.

Hours reading	4	13	20	9	18	1	11	8	18	2	15	10	4	14	7
Spelling test score	6	12	20	8	17	2	13	10	19	3	16	12	5	12	7

   a Draw a scatter graph to show this data. Draw each axis with a scale from 0 to 25. Take the horizontal axis as 'Hours reading' and the vertical axis as 'Spelling test score'.
   b What type of correlation does the scatter graph show? Explain your answer.

2. The table shows the art and science exam results of 15 students. The results for both subjects are given as percentages.

Art result	72	34	81	57	32	78	65	67	53	61	35	42	55	79	31
Science result	27	62	19	41	66	25	37	32	59	48	63	59	40	35	77

   a Draw a scatter graph to show this data. Draw each axis with a scale from 0 to 100. Take the horizontal axis as 'Art result' and the vertical axis as 'Science result'.
   b What type of correlation does the scatter graph show? Explain your answer.

3. The table shows the number of packets of biscuits and the number of packets of crisps sold by a grocery store each day over a period of 10 days.

Number of packets of biscuits sold	15	12	26	22	8	25	16	14	9	28
Number of packets of crisps sold	12	22	14	7	28	27	25	18	17	25

   a Draw a scatter graph to show this data. Take the horizontal axis as 'Number of packets of biscuits sold' with a scale from 0 to 30. Take the vertical axis as 'Number of packets of crisps sold' with a scale from 0 to 30.
   b What type of correlation does the scatter graph show? Explain your answer.

4. The scatter graph shows the value of two-bedroom houses in a town and the distance of the houses from the railway station.

   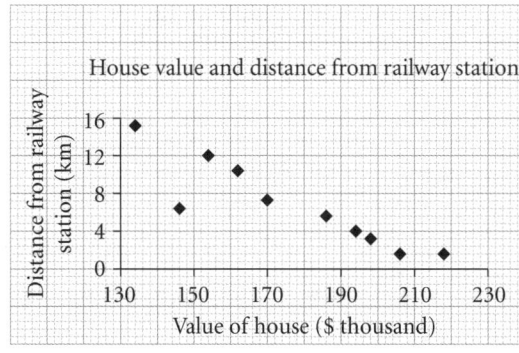

   a What type of correlation does the scatter graph show? Explain your answer.
   b One of the houses does not seem to fit the correlation. Which house is this?
      Explain why you think this house may be different from the others.

◆ Exercise 19.4 Interpreting and drawing stem-and-leaf diagrams

1 The owner of a horse-riding school records the numbers of customers she has each day over a two-week period in June and a two-week period in August.
The tables show her results.

Number of customers during two weeks in June

43	37	45	68	39	20	43
40	60	46	42	46	41	46

Number of customers during two weeks in August

47	55	62	38	36	50	43
54	37	58	40	58	52	56

a Draw a back-to-back stem-and-leaf diagram to show this data.
b For both months work out:
  i the mode   **ii** the median   **iii** the range   **iv** the mean.
c Compare and comment on the numbers of customers during the different months.
d The owner of the horse-riding school thinks that she has more customers, on average, in August. Do you agree? Explain your answer.

2 The stem-and-leaf diagram shows the times taken by the students in a stage 9 class to complete a word puzzle.

```
         Girls' times              Boys' times
                          9 | 24 |
          6  5  5  4  2  1 | 25 | 3
                8  4  3  1  0 | 26 | 2  5  5  5  8
                      5  3  3  3 | 27 | 1  3  5  6  7  7  9
                                 | 28 | 6  8  9
```

Key: For the girls' times, 9 | 24 means 24.9 seconds
For the boys' times, 25 | 3 means 25.3 seconds

a For both sets of times, work out:
  i the mode   **ii** the median   **iii** the range   **iv** the mean.
b Compare and comment on the times taken by the girls and the boys to complete the word puzzle.

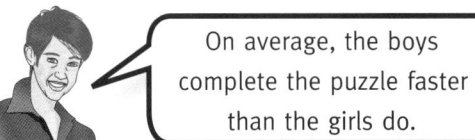

On average, the boys complete the puzzle faster than the girls do.

On average, the girls complete the puzzle faster than the boys do.

c Read what Shen says. Which average do you think he is using?
d Read what Tanesha says. Which average do you think she is using?
e Who do you think are faster at completing the puzzle, the girls or the boys? Explain your answer.

3 The figures below show the number of boxes of cereal sold in a supermarket per day over a two-week period, when the cereal was on display on the top shelf and on the middle shelf.

Top shelf

109	125	128	112	119	126	104
112	127	129	122	130	124	120

Middle shelf

120	142	139	145	127	115	139
136	129	144	130	147	132	138

a Draw a back-to-back stem-and-leaf diagram to show this data.
b Do you think that sales of the cereal were better when the cereal was on the top shelf or the middle shelf? Explain your answer clearly.

Exercise 19.5 Comparing distributions and drawing conclusions

1 The frequency polygons show the lengths of time that 100 cars were parked in a car park on a Wednesday and a Saturday.

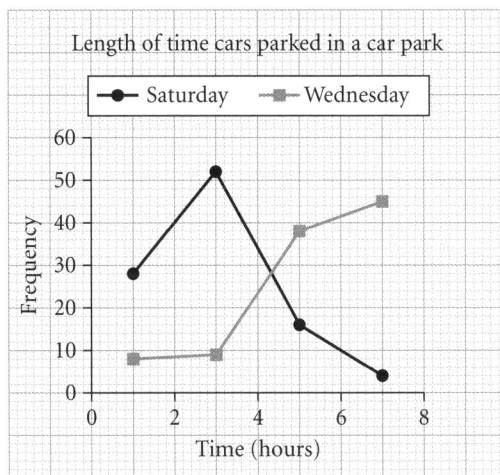

Look at the shape of the distributions.
Write three sentences that compare the lengths of time the cars were parked.

2 At an airport check-in desk the masses of 100 suitcases were recorded.
Fifty of the suitcases were being taken from the UK to Spain.
The other fifty were being taken from the UK to Sweden.
The frequency diagrams show the masses of the suitcases.

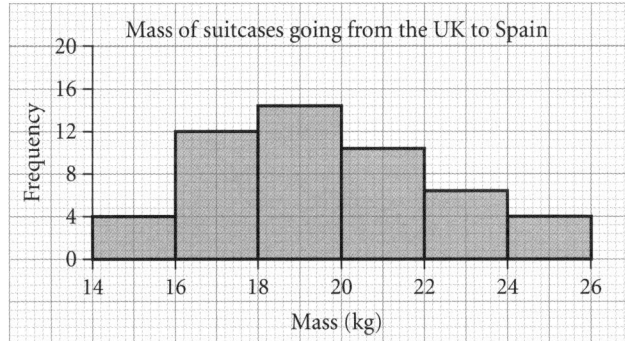
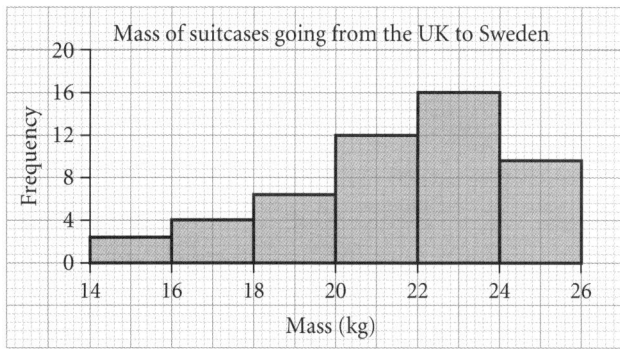

Look at the shape of the distributions. Write three sentences that compare the mass of the suitcases going from the UK to Spain and the UK to Sweden.

3 The scatter graph shows the results for class 9T in two Spanish tests, a listening test and a writing test.

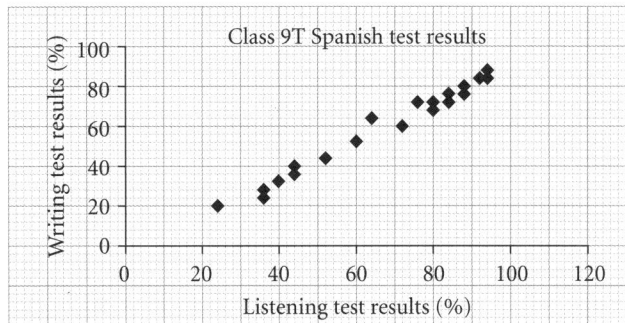

a Mr Garcia says the students who are good at listening are also good at writing.
Is Mr Garcia correct?
Explain your answer.

b One of the students, Isobel, got 64% in her listening test, but missed her writing test.
Mr Garcia thinks that Isobel would have scored about 44% in her writing test.
Do you agree?
Explain your answer.

4 The table shows the ages of the members of two tennis teams at a competition.

Team A	17	24	16	20	32	18	25	18
Team B	24	28	27	25	31	29	28	26

Steph says that, on average, team A are younger and more similar in age than team B.
Is Steph correct?
Explain your answer.